Hiding in Plain Sight

What Language Says About Being Human

Hiding in Plain Sight

What Language Says About Being Human

Serghei Sadohin

IFF
BOOKS

London, UK
Washington, DC, USA

CollectiveInk

First published by iff Books, 2024
iff Books is an imprint of Collective Ink Ltd.,
Unit 11, Shepperton House, 89 Shepperton Road, London, N1 3DF
office@collectiveinkbooks.com
www.collectiveinkbooks.com
www.iff-books.com

For distributor details and how to order please visit the 'Ordering' section on our website.

ISBN: 978 1 80341 597 0
978 1 80341 599 4 (ebook)
Library of Congress Control Number: 2023939858

A CIP catalogue record for this book is available from the British Library.

Design: Lapiz Digital Services

UK: Printed and bound by CPI Group (UK) Ltd, Croydon, CR0 4YY
Printed in North America by CPI GPS partners

We operate a distinctive and ethical publishing philosophy in all areas of our business, from our global network of authors to production and worldwide distribution.

Contents

One does not inhabit a country; one inhabits a language. That is our country, our fatherland — and no other.
Emil Cioran

The Resonance of Words

Words are clamor-filled shells. There's many a story in the miniature of a single word!

—Gaston Bachelard

What drives us humans to call ourselves 'person'? In Ancient Rome's theatre, actors wore masks, enhancing the drama of their roles, known as *dramatis personae*. These masks not only intensified visuals but, more importantly, resonated the actor's voice within their hollows. Thus, *per sonare* signifies 'to sound through'.

A person is one through whom sound reverberates. Sound of what, you wonder? Perhaps music? Indeed, as we dance to music, we embody persona, the sound enveloping us completely. In dance, we become the mask, music personified. Yet, beyond dancing, we constantly sway to an unseen rhythm. A force guides our thoughts, movements, and actions daily, everywhere, ceaselessly. That force is the sound of language. Words hum inside our minds, and even as we ponder nothing, we define it as something; a something formed in words.

In this book, we'll journey into language's intricate realms. As language conceals itself in the open, we'll unveil the hidden significance behind everyday words. Etymology, as the Greeks who coined it understood, denotes the study of the 'true essence of words'. To think originally is to think of origins, which is precisely our aim in this book.

The first part explores language's role in our world experience. In the second part, we reflect on time as the essence of being and its connection to language. Finally, the third part uncovers the various nuanced forms language has assumed throughout history, profoundly shaping our societies in often unacknowledged ways.

Diving into the sea of speech, let's navigate the currents of connection. Rekindle the lost art of listening.

Part I Through the Persona

The Great Conspiracy

For where two or three gather in my name, there am I with them.
(Matthew 18:20)

In Fyodor Dostoevsky's final and possibly greatest novel, *The Brothers Karamazov*, a curious event unfolds in the intriguing fable of the Grand Inquisitor. Set amid the Spanish Inquisition, Christ returns to earth after a fifteen-century absence, only to be arrested by the mortal Grand Inquisitor. Confined to a dungeon, Christ is ordered to remain silent. Contrary to his title, the Grand Inquisitor shows no interest in inquiry; instead, he speaks without listening, rejecting dialogue with the divine and dismissing any response. He demands that Christ leave and never return.

This peculiar tale may initially seem to convey the Inquisitor's desire to preserve the Church's authority on earth by thwarting divine interference in worldly affairs. However, the Grand Inquisitor embodies more than mere tyranny; he is a subtle genius and a benefactor to humankind. A high-ranking church official, he likely understood the profound implications of Christ's suffering and Crucifixion as the ultimate martyrdom. In Greek, *martys* signifies 'witness', and as the preeminent martyr, Christ bore divine witness for all.

The Grand Inquisitor's brilliance in banishing Christ lies in subjecting Him to an incomprehensible level of suffering: complete excommunication. He interprets the idea behind *martys* to the very end, deeming non-being an even greater martyrdom than enduring pain and death. This paradox posits that Christ had to be utterly forgotten to exist appropriately as a witness everywhere and at all times. Christ had to be nowhere to be everywhere. He had to be nothing to be everything. In other words, he had to hide in plain sight.

5

But where does the divine spirit ultimately hide? Within the Word. Existing as and within the Word of mortals such as the Grand Inquisitor who, fittingly, refused to inquire but merely expressed himself, Christ remains silent. His witness resonates through every persona, omnipresent yet concealed, silent yet vocal; looking at us directly but saying nothing. He is sought but never found. For Dostoevsky, God does not need to in-sist by coming to earth himself; he already and always ex-sists, that is 'stands forth'[1] and behind every human word and deed. The Word, the logos, precedes and incorporates God in itself, with its origins enshrouded in a mysterious conspiracy.

In the depths of history lies this grand conspiracy we partake in daily; one that unites and divides us: language. A whispered union, the term conspiracy itself is derived from the Latin *conspirare* (breathing together), exemplifying the essence of this double-edged linguistic dance. As the essence of the human spirit, language intertwines our breaths as one while at the same time cultivating seeds of discord.

The ancient story of the Tower of Babel captures the essence of this enigmatic conspiracy. Once, humanity collaborated to approach the divine, constructing a tower to pierce the heavens. But God intervened, confounding their speech and scattering them into a cacophony of unfamiliar languages. Formerly united architects now saw one another as alien, even charging their counterparts with barbarism upon hearing their incomprehensible utterances (*bar bar; bla bla*).[2] Thus, the Tower of Babel transmuted into the Tower of babbling, an emblem of our capacity to both connect and confound.

While definitive theories on the genesis of language elude us, the crux lies in its development and role within human history. Historians like Yuval Noah Harari argue that history began with language, shaping us into Homo sapiens around seventy thousand years ago.[3] The cognitive revolution and human history sprouted from our ability to weave tales of our origins through language.

Linguist Daniel Everett suggests an even earlier origin with Homo erectus: over a million years ago when tools entered the picture. Everett highlights that culture involves 'symbolic reasoning and projecting meaning onto the world',[4] transforming things into symbols imbued with meaning. Later we will explore how everything in our world becomes a shared symbol, moulded through discussion on 'things'.

While pinpointing the exact emergence of language remains a challenge, the focus of our exploration lies in how it functions in human society and the connection we share with it. The pivotal question is whether we shape language or language shapes us. Throughout this book, we champion the latter idea.

Language lacks a singular origin. While the Bible ascribes God's genesis to the Word (John 1:1), the source and meaning of that word remain elusive. Language is a collective undertaking, with words exchanged in communication. As social beings, humans perceive themselves within communities based on *communication*. Thus, it is not the lone individual, but the whole community that engages in the act of communicating. Hans-Georg Gadamer astutely observed, 'Whoever speaks a language that no one else understands does not speak. To speak means to speak to someone.'[5]

The enigmatic nature of language, as a spontaneous gift from the ether, captivates the human spirit. Wilhelm von Humboldt, a German linguist and philosopher, marvelled at the might of language, dwarfing individual power: 'Language wells from a depth of human existence which prohibits regarding it generally as a labour and as a creation of peoples. It possesses an evident spontaneity [...], hence it is not a labour of nations, but rather a gift fallen to them as a result of their innate destiny. They make use of it without knowing how they produced it.'[6] While Nietzsche discerned that consciousness is moulded not by rationality, but by the linguistic rhythm. Speaking reigns supreme, transcending mere thinking.

In *We Philologists*, Nietzsche, the philologist, embraced his role as an interpreter of language. Michel Foucault encapsulated Nietzsche's philosophy as an exegesis of Greek words,[7] highlighting his fascination with language's musicality. In Nietzsche's realm, music assumes the throne, the ultimate expression of existence, surpassing all else. As we venture forth, we'll discover that music and language stem from common origins.

Dwelling in Words

Let no one say that I have said nothing new; the arrangement of the subject is new. When we play tennis, we both play with the same ball, but one of us places it better.

—Pascal

Language is not thought; it simply is. It is a given. Speaking and thinking move together in harmony. French philosopher Maurice Merleau-Ponty contends that language is not a mere instrument for expressing thoughts but a means of actualizing them.[8] Genuine thinking emerges only when thoughts find verbal expression. Even silent thinking resonates with language, as our ability to think depends on our capacity to articulate.

Martin Heidegger, known for his wordplay, demonstrates this in his essay *What is called thinking?* Already within the title's question, he reveals the answer: thinking is the act of calling it into existence and expressing it through language. 'To call is not originally to name', he says, 'but the other way around, naming is a kind of calling.'[9] Creative individuals, such as writers and poets, recognize that their works emerge from calling forth their thoughts and housing them in words. It is, as the saying goes, their *calling* to do so. 'The author is dead', Roland Barthes famously proclaimed, regarding the author himself as a mere persona: a conduit or messenger through which thoughts are conveyed.

Our thoughts, like people, bear names. Baptizing thoughts with words is the essence of thinking. It is telling that thinking (*denken*) and thanking (*danken*) are connected in German and English. When we think, we thank ourselves for creating those thoughts; or rather, thoughts themselves thank us for bringing them forth into being. Heidegger believed poets were the true thinkers, surpassing professional philosophers like himself. Our streets and squares often adopt their names as tokens of gratitude for their musings. Make way, Homo sapiens, and hail the Homo poeticus!

At its core, even philosophy is about understanding the world by lending an ear to language itself. As Wittgenstein noted, we must battle the bewitchment of our intelligence by language and against language to truly comprehend the world around us.[10] To further explore this idea, let's examine the connection between language and human consciousness by decoding its etymological meaning: *com* (with, together) + *scire* (knowledge) equals 'collective knowledge'. To make sense of things, we must use, as we say, *common sense*. Without a community and its communication, human consciousness wouldn't exist.

Had Adam never conversed with Eve, would he have become conscious? Scripture states, 'And Adam knew Eve his wife; and she conceived, and bare Cain, and said, I have gotten a man from the LORD' (Genesis 4:1). The term 'knew' and Eve's utterance 'and said' disclose a bond between consciousness and language. As Humboldt asserts, 'The "thou" is an automatic counterpart of the "I."'[11] What stands between them is the common sense of language.

Language influences not only our thinking but also our physiological existence as a persona. Literary critic and linguist George Steiner, who studied the relationship between language and human development, proposes that language may have even preceded the development of a central nervous system in humans and contributed significantly to the selection of variants most adept at utilizing its resources.[12] In essence, language may have played a role in creating humans, rather than the other way around.

Words, like keys on a piano, stir emotions and ease the mind, harmonizing the unspoken complexity of existence. They streamline the mental and physical effort required to understand and navigate our surroundings. A simple word like 'air' saves us from the laborious task of resorting to gestures to convey the concept of something essential yet invisible.

As the personae through which language reverberates, we sift and interpret the world in a symphony of perception. Each word strikes a note, a metaphor, Greek for 'to transfer'. Words shape our comprehension, moulding it into signs our minds can grasp and internalize. Marshall McLuhan stated that 'all words are metaphor (except, in a special sense, the word 'word' itself)'.[13] In this context, the word 'word' is ironically unique, as it represents the foundational concept of language without resorting to metaphor. In the Bible, it was the Word, the non-metaphoric one, that existed from the very beginning, and without it, no other words could exist. Meaning emerges as linguistic signs and metaphors harmonize, and language becomes an unending, cosmic poem.

A tapestry woven from metaphor, it shapes our cosmic dance with existence, as Lakoff and Johnson elucidate in *Metaphors We Live By*. Metaphors transcend mere poetry, pervading every linguistic fabric, from love, time, space, and morality to our very sense of self. Even unassuming prepositions, like 'in', carry metaphorical weight, pre-positioning our place in the world. Lakoff and Johnson spotlight the 'container metaphor', in which 'in' evokes containment: be it milk in a glass, a book in a room, or a soul in love. Language orchestrates our thoughts through prepositions, aligning us with the world around and offering a compass to navigate existence.

As we say we exist 'in nature', we might envision nature as a container. Yet, this view is misleading. Instead, focus on the prefix ex- in *ex-sistere*, which speaks of emergence, appearance, or coming forth, as if from a state of non-existence or non-being into being (akin to the familiar *ex-nihilo*). In other words, 'ex-' indicates that something is understood out of itself, not being 'placed' within something else. Human existence, thus, is a self-interpretation, a self-transfer of meaning, of oneself in the world. Language, our steadfast guide in this circular interpretation, shines the way.

Lakoff and Johnson propose that the metaphorical use of prepositions in language originates from our embodied experience of being bounded by our skin, which shapes our perception of the world. As physical beings, we project our in-out orientation onto other objects in our environment. This container metaphor, derived from our own bodies, is particularly evident in the German language, where the words for 'house' (*haus*) and 'skin' (*haut*) are nearly identical.

The metaphorical use of prepositions is also essential in understanding human desire for sex. Words like 'intimacy' reveal the profound meaning of the preposition 'in', which our physical bodies poetize through metaphoric language. Sex transcends a mere physical act, becoming a conversation between two bodies: an intimate, wordless dialogue.[14] Love, too, is not merely an emotion but a communicative act, as German sociologist Niklas Luhmann observes in *Love as Passion*. Love, Luhmann writes, is 'a code of communication according to the rules of which one can express, form and simulate feelings, deny them, impute them to others, and be prepared to face up to all the consequences which enacting such a communication may bring with it'.[15] In other words, love is a performance of the persona, which almost always happens to be a dramatic one.

In each cultural epoch, every language crafts its distinct code for love, shaping the medium through which this emotion reverberates. Tolstoy's *War and Peace* elucidates the significance of love as a communicative code, a channel that influences the manner in which love is expressed and experienced. In an insightful episode, Tolstoy discerns authentic 'love' from mere 'communication on love'. We witness Pierre Bezukhov, one of Russia's wealthiest men, convinced that he loves the enchanting Helene Kuragina, a woman of high esteem in St Petersburg's elite circles. The scene unfolds as Pierre hesitates in confessing his love:

> 'Helene!' he said aloud and paused.
> 'Something special is always said in such cases', he thought, but could not remember what it was that people say. He looked at her face. She drew nearer to him. Her face flushed. [...]
> 'It is too late now, it's done; besides I love her', thought Pierre.
> '*Je vous aime!* (I love you)' he said, remembering what has to be said at such moments: but his words sounded so weak that he felt ashamed of himself.'[16]

Pierre's reliance on recalling 'what it was that people say' demonstrates his adherence to a code, rather than following his heart. He expresses his love in French, rather than his native Russian, the words sounding weak even to his ears. Pierre senses something amiss, but he continues to follow the code. A peculiar and invisible social force seems to constrain him, but he remains uncertain of its nature.[17]

The quest for love and sexual attraction played an essential role in developing our language and communication skills throughout history, slowly changing the shape of our bodies. As humans became better communicators, they no longer needed large physical size or sharp canines to fight.[18] Instead, sexual selection favoured a sharper and more poetic tongue. In the captivating tale of Orpheus from Ovid's *Metamorphoses*, women are irresistibly drawn to the virtuoso bard, whose way with words ignites passions and desires. 'Orpheus now would have nothing to do with the love of women, perhaps because of his fortune in love, or he may have plighted his troth for ever. But scores of women were burning to sleep with the bard and suffered the pain of rejection' (10.79–85). Ovid later illustrates how Orpheus, uninterested in their affections, inadvertently incites their wrath, leading to a shocking climax of orgiastic violence leading to the poet's tragic murder. The tale underscores the magnetic allure of poetic language and its profound impact on human connection and desire.

Essentially, language serves as a means for the body to express itself, and it is only through language that we can truly comprehend its desires. Cioran's question, 'This body — what use is it, if not to make us understand the meaning of the word *torturer*?'[19] highlights the idea that our bodies communicate messages through language. It is not the body that understands language, but rather language that interprets the body's complexities.

Envision the human body as the primary physical vessel for our existence 'in' the world, a notion that might be illusory, and language as the metaphysical counterpart. Heidegger dubbed language 'the house of Being', illustrating our existence and dwelling within the logos.[20] The rooms of this house, our words, paint a vivid picture of the physical world. This intricate interplay between body and language reveals that language doesn't just shape our thoughts, feelings, and position in the world, but also our physiology, even before we consciously engage with it. We don't adopt language; language adopts us, and as soon as we tune into its rhythm, we unveil the true power of language in choreographing human experience.

Obeying the Vernacular

My sheep hear my voice, and I know them, and they follow me.
(John 10:27)

The tale of Odysseus and his encounter with the sirens in Greek mythology, as well as the biblical story of the Apostle Stephen, both involve the protagonists struggling against the alluring power of spoken words. Odysseus had his crew plug their ears with beeswax and tie him to the ship's mast so he could listen to the sirens' enchanting songs without succumbing to their influence. Meanwhile, Stephen's words were so captivating that his detractors were forced to cover their ears and shout to avoid being swayed by his speech. 'Behold, I see the heavens opened, and the Son of man standing on the right hand of God.' As he described the glorious scene upon which his eyes were gazing, it was more than his persecutors could endure. Stopping their ears, that they might not hear his words, and uttering loud cries, they ran furiously upon him with one accord 'and cast him out of the city' (Acts 7:56).

The interplay between language and obedience is illuminated by the ancient Greek and Hebrew concept of 'hearing', which also signified 'obeying'.[21] This semantic bond between hearing and obeying underpins language's power to influence. When we first learn language, we tune into its sounds before embracing its written form. The term 'language' itself originates from *lingua*, denoting tongue, speech, or voice.

Swept up by the rhythm of language, we instinctively submit and comply. The vernacular of our early years imprints itself upon us, compelling us to adopt the role of *verna*, or 'home-born slaves', as hinted in the word *vernaculus*. Language offers no alternative but to obey. This unspoken pact of adherence to a shared language resonates through generations, primarily aurally rather than in written form.

From our earliest moments as beings unable to speak (the very essence of *infans* in its Latin roots), we embark on a linguistic odyssey through babble. However, these babbles never find a place in our shared language lexicon. To permit each newborn to integrate their own babbles into a language would generate chaos akin to the Tower of Babel. To preserve order, the logos assumes command, coercing us to involuntarily submit to its authority from the very beginning. In this manner, words act as our passports into the realm of adulthood, tethering us to the dominion of language and its potent sway over our thoughts and actions.

As children, we never genuinely utter 'a first word', as that word belongs to the public domain of language always and already. Words predate both us and our deities; we merely surrender to their supremacy. We adhere to our elders when they tell us that a 'tree' is pronounced as 'tree' and not 'tla' or 'tlee'. In essence, our compliance serves not to appease our parents but to uphold the integrity of language itself. We become its involuntary protectors, regardless of our intentions, signifying that language rules over us all rather than being controlled by any individual.

The intrinsic semantic bond between hearing and obeying is not exclusive to Hebrew and Greek; a close examination of all European languages reveals this connection.[22] Within the Latin origins of the word 'to obey', *ob-audire*, meaning 'hearing towards', we find the message that language communicates to us: upon hearing it, we must obey and belong to it, devoid of any choice. As Blaise Pascal asserts, *Fides ex auditu* 'faith comes by hearing'.[23] If we seek sound evidence for this, we notice that the evidence is, in fact, sound.

Language's ultimate author is both everyone and no one simultaneously. The true origin lies in the Word itself, the autonomous entity present at the inception of everything and everyone. Yet, one word holds unparalleled sovereignty. It is the supreme deity of all words, and in the Old Testament, the Hebrews named it Yahweh, meaning 'I am who I am', or simply 'Being'. This singular verb resides at the core of language and, consequently, our entire existence as human beings. It could be argued that without the verb 'to be', the world itself could not exist as it reveals to us in its full splendour.

The Most Interesting Word

Before the earth and the sea
and the all-encompassing heaven
came into being, the whole of nature
displayed but a single face,
which men have called Chaos.

—Ovid

The most interesting word? Concealing inter-essences, it glides between essence and essence, revealing itself as being. If language were a melody, it would sing 'being'. Yet, how does one grasp such an elusive concept? One may wander amid essences, only to return to the word itself. 'In the beginning was the Word', proclaims the Bible. 'And the word was with God. And the word was God.' What word could possibly precede the divine? What first utterance sprang from a caveman's lips, rippling like an echo, resonating like an echo, transforming him from an indistinct object to a conscious subject: the self-aware 'I am', 'I exist'? As with all things genuinely interesting, the answer hides between essences — in the beginning, the word: *was*. All the roads lead to Rome, but in the language of human beings, all the roads lead to being.

Every living creature on our planet communicates. To survive is to maintain at least minimal communication with the outside world. From bacteria to trees, fish, and mammals, all living organisms interact within a complex, interdependent system known as an ecosystem. Nature's main attribute is its idyllic unity, a level of perfection beyond human comprehension, which often makes us feel like intruders.

However, our language is not merely another form of communication among living creatures. Human language possesses a unique concept of being, absent in other life forms. This single concept makes our language far more complex than any other communicative system, setting it apart entirely. The word 'to be' forms the foundation of our language and existence, enabling us to understand and connect with the world around us.

As humans, we ex-sist; we emerge, we appear in nature, within and towards ourselves. A unique, interesting dance between the self and nature, being forms an unbreakable bond. Neither nature nor humanity stands alone — being, the silent force, weaves them into harmony.

'Man is the shepherd of Being', Heidegger claims, for we alone confront, nurture, and wrestle with our existence. Unlike other creatures that simply 'live', humans uniquely 'be' and 'become' in the true sense of the word. To be or not to be? Hamlet's famed dilemma reflects our power to choose, our privilege to shape the course of our lives. As guardians of existence, we entwine our destiny with the fabric of being, creating a captivating tapestry.

In both the Greco-Roman world and the biblical narrative, the creation of the world involves a separation or distinction of elements, breaking the oneness of chaos. The word 'to be' fractures this oneness in our human world, making it more complex and beautiful by tying it back together into a unity of being. Thanks to the magic of the verb 'to be', we can distinguish individual elements, like a leaf from a tree, and perceive them as separate entities that 'emerge' in nature.

However, the being of the tree, the leaf, or anything else conceals a crucial aspect of the equation that often escapes our attention. This aspect is not about the external world of nature, but about our relationship with it. The first being that emerges from this world of chaos is the existing human being.

For the great Roman poet Ovid, the world's creation began when the oneness of chaos and the void started to be fractured into different beings by the god of nature. A single unified nothing began to take form and disintegrate into various somethings coming into being:

> The god who is nature was kinder and
> brought this dispute to a settlement.
> He severed the earth from the sky and he
> parted the sea from the land;
> he separated translucent space from the
> cloudier atmosphere.
> He disentangled the elements, so as to set
> them free
> from the heap of darkness, then gave them
> their separate places and tied them
> down in a peaceful concordat.

Biblical God Yahweh, architect of difference, dissolves chaos by dividing day from night. In this act, the Word, the very essence of 'to be', shatters nature's unity, rekindling harmony; what Ovid calls here 'peaceful concordat'.

In nature, a leaf is an element of a tree's wholeness yet discrete from the tree itself. But only for us. Courtesy of the enchantment of the verb 'to be', we extract the leaf from the tree and perceive it as a being of its own; that is a separate being from the entirety of magnificent beingness. This word is akin to a magical brush, bestowing upon us a vivid world and interrupting the uniformity of nature that our animal brethren dwell in. We might even propose that while animals reside in chaos, humans inhabit the orderly entente of being, encompassing all its individual beings within itself. In the realm of being, chaos cedes to order.

Yet, the equation's overlooked element lies not in nature but within ourselves. From chaos emerges the first being: the existing human. Ovid continues:

Although the land and the sea and the sky were
involved in the great mass,
no one could stand on the land or swim in the
waves of the sea, and the sky had no light.
None of the elements kept its shape,
and all were in conflict inside one body: the cold
with the hot, the wet with the dry, the soft with the hard, and
weight with the weightless.

Who is supposed to stand on the land, swim in the waves of the sea, and bring shape to all the elements in nature? The poet clarifies that it is humans themselves:

Nature had hardly been settled within its separate
compartments
when stars, which had long been hidden inside
the welter of Chaos,
began to explode with light all over the vault of the
heavens.
And lest any part of the world should be wanting its
own living creatures,
the floor of heaven was richly inlaid with the stars
and the planets,
the waves of the sea were assigned as the realm of
the glinting fishes,
the earth was the home of the beasts, and the
yielding air of the birds.
Yet a holier living creature, more able to think high

thoughts,
which could hold dominion over the rest, was still
to be found.
So Man came into the world.

Distinct from nature's unity, human understanding of being severs our oneness with it. An eternal observer, humanity can befriend nature at best but never rejoin its essence. The dilemma Adam and Eve endured was the mandatory separation from Eden's sanctuary to attain a conscious human identity. Their first attempt at clothing represented an initial imposition of order upon nature, starting with their own bodies. They emerged as what we generally call *subjects* — the 'thrown under' — a testament to their newfound self-consciousness and self-awareness.

Blame not technology for environmental destruction, but the word 'is'. Yet, can our existence truly be nature's original sin? Without humanity, the world would simply cease to be an order, neither good nor bad. Nietzsche asserts that terms like 'good' and 'bad' hold meaning only for humans.[24] For nature to have meaning, the human being must be.

Dostoevsky's passage implies that it might indeed be unjust for us to exist in this world: 'If I have once been given to understand and realize that *I am* — what does it matter to me that the world is organized on a system full of errors and that otherwise it cannot be organized at all? Who will or can judge me after this? Say what you like — the thing is impossible and unjust!'[25] It might indeed be unjust to nature's harmony that we impose our own order by means of 'destruction'. However, there is no other way for humans to exist than to simply be: the very essence of that original destruction.

Living in a forest instead of a city doesn't make us wholly 'one' with nature. Anthropologist Claude Levi-Strauss contends that nature isn't independent but is an interpretation shaped by various cultures: 'In the first place, natural conditions are not passively submitted to. What is more, they have no existence on their own, since they are a function of the technology and way of life of the population that defines them and gives them a meaning by exploiting them in a given direction. Nature is not contradictory in itself; it can be contradictory only in terms of the particular human activity that takes place within it.'[26] What is that activity that is contra-dictory within nature? It is the human activity of con-diction (*con dicare*), the speaking together, which makes up the natural condition. We can't discuss natural conditions without acknowledging and indicating their cultural context. Nature, derived from the Latin word *natus*, signifies birth, and it is within nature that we, humans, are born. 'Nature has made all her truths independent of one another', writes Pascal. 'Our art makes one dependent on the other. But this is not natural. Each keeps its own place.'

In contemplating a global scenario absent of human presence, one is compelled to adopt the perspective of an uninvolved, celestial spectator, akin to a divine being, beholding a paradisiacal earth devoid of humanity. However, such an abstraction borders on the realms of the fantastical, for the concept of 'nature in isolation' is itself a fallacy. When we assign the verb 'to be' to nature, we are inadvertently imposing our own human structures and systems upon it. Consequently, to omit ourselves from the equation is to wilfully disregard an intrinsic, symbiotic essence that holds profound significance: our very selves. Envisioning our own nonexistence, or the existence of the world sans humanity, is an exercise in futility. As Cioran elucidates: 'I strive to conceive the cosmos without ... myself. Fortunately, death is here to remedy my imagination's inadequacy.'[27]

And acknowledging our part in this grand tapestry isn't vain or human-cantered. The problem doesn't lie in our existence but in how it manifests for us, and how we emerge to it, and it emerges to us. We can opt to be ecological, responsible, inventive, and moderate in living harmoniously with nature. In other words, we can always *be* different. Language, our trusty companion, plays a starring role in our condition. As Bachelard puts it, 'to speak well is part of living well.' Evading our own being proves futile, but beware, being can deceive us in return. Once again, by means of language.

Nature Loves to Hide

A word, once dissected, no longer signifies anything, is nothing. Like a body that, after the autopsy, is less than a corpse.

—Cioran

The verb 'to be' delineates the human condition, setting us apart from nature. In our quest for belonging, we seek a home amidst the living. While animals find shelters, they do not have homes. Our existence, eternally questioning, propels us to establish a haven within the world. The human, while longing for being, always seeks be-longing: somewhere, sometime, and somehow. He fabricates walls, fences, borders, and clothes, creating boundaries to foster a sense of here, rather than there or anywhere. Our skin, the primordial demarcation of being, underscores our perpetual state of 'somewhere'. An animal roams as anyone; we, however, are always someone. It lingers in no time; we are always sometime. It lives for life and survival; we live to be and become. Though seemingly ambiguous, 'to be' firmly anchors us in the concrete realm of being, the most resolute word of all.

And this is why pinning down 'being' is no simple feat. It's not the same as 'life', for animals have life but lack being. Early Greek pre-Socratic philosophers, like Parmenides and Heraclitus, wrestled with defining being, and their inquiries still challenge us today.

Heraclitus, in ancient wisdom, declared, 'Nature loves to hide.' Throughout the ages, philosophy and science of the West have endeavoured to unravel this mystery: what does nature truly conceal? Could it be hiding the human nature itself? Nature, in the guise of the veiled goddess Isis, perpetually re-veils her countenance, engaging us in an eternal game of hide-and-seek.[28] Nietzsche contemplated, 'Perhaps truth is a woman who has reasons for not showing her reasons?'[29] McLuhan's famous twentieth-century aphorism resonates with this sentiment: 'the medium is the message.' The message nestles within the invisible medium itself. The persona, the mask, becomes the medium through which the hidden message of being resonates. But what is the most evident is the most unnoticed.

Our pursuit of nature's enigmas is, at its essence, an exploration of our connection with the elusive deity and our unfolding within her realm. As nature shrouds its secrets, so too does the concept of being find refuge within language and thought.

Defining being becomes an intricate interplay, guiding us towards the seemingly illogical yet compelling conclusion that being equates to nothingness. The paradox that emerges — how can being signify nothing, when the word itself implies 'not-nothing'? — entangles us in a web of contradictions. Yet, within this paradox lies a treasure trove of insight about language.

Take for instance the simple phrase 'a thing is'. While we fixate on the 'thing', we often overlook the 'is', deeming it self-evident and trivial. It's the difficulty of posing the seemingly oxymoronic question, 'What is "is"?' that allows being to slip our attention, making it seem unquestionable and self-evident. As Aristotle noted, 'For as the eyes of bats are to the blaze of day, so is the reason in our soul to the things which are by nature most evident of all.'[30]

If a thing exists in being, does that imply being itself is also a thing? To equate being with a thing would be tautological.

We ask, 'Why something is', not 'Why is "is"?' This distinction highlights that a thing and its being have complementary yet distinct meanings. Therefore, the thing exists precisely because 'is' cannot be a thing, leading to the conclusion that being is, indeed, no-thing.

In his work *Metaphysics*, Aristotle was among the first philosophers to systematically study the concept of being. He argued that philosophers, not scientists or theologians, are the ones who concern themselves with understanding the essence of this word. Recognizing that being has multiple meanings, Aristotle acknowledged that no practical, productive, or theoretical science troubles itself about it.[31] This idea leads us to consider the seemingly absurd and unpractical questions philosophers address, such as 'What is "is"?' And why is this 'is' — *nothing at all*?

'In the beginning was the Word', states the biblical phrase, evading the specification of the Word's nature. Specifying a form for the Word would've made it a something distinct, yet it remains undefined, an unidentifiable nothingness. Still, even as an empty word, it persists as the Word; the Word that somehow, already, *was*.

Does this suggest the world's origin in absurdity? Possibly, but not as we conventionally grasp the term. *Absurdum*, translated as 'out of tune' or literally 'not deaf', demands our attentive listening to what is being said. And what is being said is *already* being itself: the message finds itself as the hidden medium. Inextricably linked, being and language coalesce; it matters not what is said, as long as it is uttered. Yet, we cannot confine 'it' to a particular 'thing'. By definition, to define something means to find its contours, its finitude. Hence being cannot be defined, since it always transcends the contours of any and every particular thing.

Even in divine contemplation, we must resist reducing God to a mere thing. Aristotle's reference to God as 'the most excellent of things' demonstrates that nature's hide-and-seek game can ensnare even the most astute intellects, including Aristotle himself. The linguistic filters, through which we interpret the world, frequently obscure the true import of language.

Merleau-Ponty suggests, 'Language is obscure in terms of its function, which is to render everything else clear. It cannot be observed or grasped directly; it can only be exercised.'[32] Recognizing language's revelatory role and discerning the enigmatic function of 'to be' prove arduous tasks. Yet, without 'to be', the human language would be unfathomable.

Foucault notes the centrality of 'to be': 'Without it, everything would have remained silent, and though men, like certain animals, would have been able to make use of their voices well enough, yet not one of those cries hurled through the jungle would ever have proved to be the first link in the great chain of language.'[33] Our expressions often presuppose being without declaring it outright, such as 'I sing' or 'I walked', instead of 'I am the one singing', and 'I am the one walking'. Thoughts and communication appear inconceivable without the implicit assumption of being.

Despite its importance, the explicit usage of 'being' fades into the background, leaving us with only its implicit influence. Interestingly, numerous languages around the globe lack a proper verb for 'to be'.[34] The Greeks, however, were gifted with this verb from the beginning, allowing them to probe its depths and explore its mysteries. Their early philosophies revolved around the question of being, which modern society has largely overlooked.

In the grand play of words, the Word emerges as the omnipresent actor, the underlying resonance in the cosmic symphony. Weaving through language, the ungraspable, ineffable Word lingers, ever elusive, challenging us to listen attentively and celebrate the interplay of language and being.

Everything Is Real

This has caused me the greatest difficulty, and continues to cause me the greatest difficulty: to bear in mind that what things are called is unspeakably more important than what they are.

—Nietzsche

Expanding on the distinction between 'being' and 'the thing', we can delve deeper into the latter to gain additional insights into the nature of our unifying medium. To probe further into the concept of 'the thing', we must explore language as the hidden medium that reveals its message in the thing itself.

'Perhaps we shall then recognize', says Nietzsche, 'that the thing in itself is worth a Homeric laugh; that it *seemed* so much, indeed everything, and is really empty, namely, empty of meaning.'[35] Heidegger supplements this idea, stating, 'we do not say what we see, but rather the reverse, we see what *one says* about the matter.'[36] The crux lies in the name we assign to the thing, for communication, or *communicare*, means sharing. Consequently, the power of words transforms everything in our world into a shared some-thing.

This notion of shared meaning naturally leads us to consider the fundamental and often overlooked word 'thing'. In English, everything originates from 'the thing'. But what exactly is a thing? Delving into this seemingly innocuous question can reveal profound insights. Etymologically, the English word 'thing' is derived from the Old Germanic word *Ding*, signifying 'meeting' or 'an assembly of people'. In Scandinavian languages, the word *ting* still denotes 'a hearing in court'. This linguistic connection suggests that every thing is contingent upon human conversation, requiring entrance into language and being named accordingly. As Everett asserts, 'Rousseau's social contract is not the first contractual foundation of human society [...]. Language is.'[37] Could it be that one of the earliest social contracts was a verbal agreement to define 'the thing' collectively?

Bruno Latour, in *We Have Never Been Modern*, echoes Michel Serres' astute observation of the roots of the word 'thing' in European languages, linked to the notion of 'cause', as seen in the French *chose* or Spanish *cosa*. Intricately woven with law, politics, and criticism, objects appear to gain existence through the deliberations of assemblies or the verdicts of juries: unnamed objects *accused* and transformed into 'things'. Thus, every 'thing' holds reality, acquiring it through the language and discourse enveloping it.

In Latin, *res* denotes 'thing', from which *realitas*, or reality, springs forth. Reality takes on a thingly character, as when we inquire, 'is this a thing now?', meaning, is this real? For the Ancients, human reality seemingly arose from tribunals. Serres asserts, 'The tribunal stages the very identity of cause and thing, of word and object, or the passage of one to the other by substitution. A thing emerges there.'

A thing, then, is the cause, but the cause resides not in the physical thing itself (the message); it dwells within the word depicting it (the medium). To attain the status of real, a thing must bear meaning, a meaning that is always shared. Augustine professed, *Rem viderunt, causam non viderunt* ('They have seen the thing, they have not seen the cause').[38]

Our perception of human 'reality' depends on language: the primary tool for being conscious of things in our shared world. Through language, we share a common reality that prevents any single person or group from monopolizing this vital human instrument. While language is undemocratic in the sense that we hear and obey it without question, it also prevents any single party or person from imposing a one-sided view on things for too long without eventually sharing the objective truth with others. Language has its own truth. In fact, it is the truth *par excellence*.

Gadamer adds, 'The meaning of the German word *Sache* (thing) is permeated by what is called *causa*, the disputed 'matter' under consideration. Originally, it was the thing placed between the disputing parties because a decision still had to be rendered. The thing was to be protected against the domineering grasp of one party or the other. In this context, objectivity means opposition to partiality, that is, to the misuse of the law for partial purposes.'[39]

Words weave the tapestry of our reality, colouring both physical and abstract worlds. When we agree on what to call things, we can navigate the world together. As Steiner suggests, truth often lies in the relationship between words and words rather than between words and things.[40] This truth becomes evident when we consider abstract ideas that exist solely within our minds, but also physical objects that we encounter every day.

Consider the 1980 South African film *The Gods Must Be Crazy*, where a Coca-Cola bottle, landing unexpectedly in a remote tribe's territory, incites confusion. The tribe members, bereft of a word to describe the bottle, concoct various purposes for it, igniting conflict. A mere word, like 'bottle', could have averted these disputes, underlining language's potency in shaping our comprehension of the world.

In our industrialized present, we may not quarrel over the functions of physical objects like bottles, but we still wrestle with abstract notions, such as 'the republic'. The Latin phrase *Res publica*, or 'the public thing', signifies a collective public reality. Within a republic, we engage in constant debates surrounding public finances, governance, and education. For instance, Brazilians designate their currency as the Real, recognizing money's abstract yet powerful nature: a ceaseless source of abstract republican contention. But where does the republic reside? Is it a specific location? Can we enter it as we would a building? No, the republic is an abstract 'real' thing, its message concealed within the medium itself: the conversation; the language of tribunals.

The unending dialogue regarding the republic breathes life into its reality. This political, invisible abode offers us a sense of belonging, a home, with some even willing to risk their lives defending it against dictatorship. Are we being foolish? We are simply being human, or, as Nietzsche would say 'all too human'.

Reality, whether physical or abstract, depends on what concerns and interests humans; nothing more, nothing less. Heidegger notes that the Latin word *res*, which signifies what is real, embodies the notion of concern for humans: 'The Roman word *res* denotes what pertains to man, concerns him and his interests in any way or manner. That which concerns man is what is real in *res*. The Roman experience of the *realitas* of *res* is that of a bearing-upon, a concern.'[41] Remarkably, when something captures our concern, it becomes real.

Our dreams, thoughts, ideas, and experiences are all real things, even if they don't exist in physical space. And what is real, after all? Is love, as an abstract thing, less real than a physical bottle? If that were the case, if only bottles existed and not this thing called love, then life would probably not be worth living at all. Without a doubt, love is the ultimate human concern, and we can even say that love is even more real than a bottle: we sing about it, compose poems, make movies, and think about love all the time. The more a concept concerns us, the more real it becomes.

In essence, as long as there is a matter with being, it finds a way to express itself meaningfully, and that way is through language. Language enables us to traverse both the physical and abstract realms, fostering a shared understanding of the world we inhabit.

Remembering Being

But the Advocate, the Holy Spirit, whom the Father will send in my name, will teach you all things and will remind you of everything I have said to you.

(John 14:26)

Being transcends mere physicality and scientific definitions. It is deeply intertwined with human language and conversation. Intriguingly, the Romans' term for 'world', *mundus*, also meant 'people'. As humans, we rely on discussions with others to comprehend the real world and all its physical elements. To be a human being means to be concerned about being, and it is this concern that connects language and human existence.

St Augustine illuminates language's power, triggering experience in mind: 'I say these words to myself, and, as I speak, there are present images of everything I am speaking of, drawn out of the same treasure-house of memory.'[42] Language re-presents being, recalling, remembering it. Augustine also emphasizes the essential role of memory in his *Confessions*: 'Great is the power of memory, an awe-inspiring mystery, my God, a power of profound and infinite multiplicity. And this is mind, this is I myself.' For Augustine, memory and identity are inseparable. Latin for identity, *idem*, means 'the same' or 'the state of being the same'; memory thus ensures that our identities remain consistent over time. In other words, we exist insofar as we remember ourselves and our experiences: 'I prefer honey to a sweet wine', the saint adds, 'a smooth taste to a rough one, not actually tasting or touching at the moment, but by recollection.'[43]

Experience unfolds in memory alone. 'Experience' (*ex-pereo*): to expire, wither. Experience, then, is not what we encounter in the present moment, but rather what has passed and transformed into memory. Bachelard muses, 'the purest happiness is the one we have lost.'[44] Happiness or sadness only emerge once we have experienced something, relinquishing it to the passage of time, turning it into *ex-sistence*, that which 'stands forth' and 'emerges' to our own selves as presence.

Language, as the indispensable aid to memory, brings expired experiences and emotions back into the present. In this way, it serves as the guardian of memory and, consequently, of everything we experience. The interplay between language and memory reveals the profound connection between being, experience, and human existence.

Imagine a world where the enchanting power of language, the warmth of love, and the clarity of truth all spring from a single, magical source: memory. It's the hidden treasure that transforms our experiences and breathes life into our relationships. The rich tapestry of Greek mythology, philosophical insights, and literary masterpieces like Dante's *Divine Comedy* unravels the intricate dance between memory and the essence of our humanity.

In ancient Greece, Mnemosyne, the goddess of memory, gifted poets and kings with the art of speech. Without the interplay between memory and language, our experiences would fade into oblivion, as if they never existed. As Kierkegaard profoundly observes, 'A life in recollection is the most perfect imaginable; memory gives you your fill more abundantly than all of reality and has a security which no reality possesses.'[45]

Enter the realm of Dante's *Divine Comedy*, an epic tale that weaves memory and love into a heart-stirring narrative. Dante's cherished memories of Beatrice guide him through Hell and Heaven, illuminating a love that transcends her physical presence. The message resonates with crystal clarity: the purest love is the most pristine memory. It is a captivating paradox that suggests our love for a person deepens in their absence, as we cherish the persona crafted through memories. As Cioran poetically states, 'When you love someone, you hope — the more closely to be attached — that a catastrophe will strike your beloved.'[46]

Love often blossoms from echoes of the past, reminiscent of someone or something we once held dear. Nietzsche brilliantly articulates this notion: 'One loves ultimately one's desires, not the thing desired.'[47] Memory, then, fuels the fire of love, as Dante so vividly portrays in his timeless poem.

In *Purgatorio*, Dante drinks from the River Lethe, the river of forgetfulness, to purify his soul before entering Heaven. Although this act necessitates forgetting past sins, Beatrice reprimands him for momentarily distancing himself from the memory of her and that of God's.[48] Dante's reliance on Beatrice's words to guide him underscores the importance of language in preserving memory.

And here, the great Florentine poet's linguistic choices unveil profound insight. *Lethe*, the Greek word for 'oblivion' or 'concealment', stands in stark contrast to *Aletheia*, the Hellenic word for 'truth', literally meaning 'unconcealment'. In this light, truth signifies the resurrection of memories from the depths of forgetfulness. Memory, Dante shows, is the lifeblood of truth, being, and love.

Modern psychology reaffirms the vital role memory plays in shaping our lives, as explored by Nobel laureate Daniel Kahneman in his book *Thinking Fast and Slow*. According to Kahneman, the 'experiencing self' and the 'remembering self' are distinct entities. While the experiencing self answers questions about the present moment, the remembering self tackles the overall experience. Our reality, as Dante, Augustine, and Kierkegaard argued, lies in recollection rather than the moment itself. Kahneman's findings support the notion that memory is our primary connection to being: 'The experiencing self is the one that answers the question: "Does it hurt now?" The remembering self is the one that answers the question: "How was it, on the whole?" Memories are all we get to keep from our experience of living, and the only perspective that we can adopt as we think about our lives is therefore that of the remembering self.'[49] This insight highlights the importance of memory in understanding our experiences in a broader context.

A cat may enjoy its meal, but it cannot answer the vital question, 'how *was* it?' This question transcends the taste of the food, encompassing our emotions, surroundings, and other factors that contribute to the overall experience. Memory captures the essence of our past, giving life its richness and meaning. A life without memories would be, for humans, an existence devoid of substance.

Language, as the vessel for memory, shapes our understanding of world experience. Jean-Paul Sartre's existentialist novel *Nausea* argues that life is nothing but a series of memorable stories we tell ourselves and others: 'For the most banal event to become an adventure, you must (and this is enough) begin to recount it. This is what fools people: a man is always a teller of tales, he lives surrounded by his stories and the stories of others, he sees everything that happens to him through them; and he tries to live his own life as if he were telling a story.'[50]

Sartre gives an account of what George Lakoff called the 'life as a journey' metaphor, where we make sense of our existence by constructing a narrative filled with highs, lows, beginnings, and endings. Our primary purpose as human beings is to weave these stories into a coherent and meaningful tapestry, making us all autobiographers, shaping our lives and memories to create a rich, intelligible narrative.

In *The Idiot*, Prince Myshkin observes: 'You may place a soldier before a cannon's mouth in battle, and fire upon him — and he will still hope. But read to that same soldier his death-sentence, and he will either go mad or burst into tears.'[51] This vivid scene underscores how words can leave a deeper impact on us than the sheer wordless events. Pronouncing a verdict (*veri dicare*) means making death a certainty. A verdict is an ultimatum: 'the last word'. The last word is all there is to life, as if life were measured not in heartbeats but in syllables.

Imagine the significance of spoken words during life's milestone moments. Can one literally *call* it a marriage if it hadn't been pronounced to be so by the priest or the civil servant? Marriage ceremonies, legal proceedings, and religious rites are all defined by the pronouncements that take place. These words don't just describe events, they transform us, bestowing new identities and altering our paths.

And what about our names? Chosen for us before birth, they give us a distinct identity even before we understand who we are. To the question 'who am I?' the first and the most straightforward answer is: I am the person behind a word, my name. Our names become the essence of our being, a constant anchor as we evolve and change. They're so precious that we protect them fiercely, as if defending the very soul of our persona.

Throughout the world, the sanctity of names and language holds deep meaning. An insult to one's name or heritage can provoke a whirlwind of emotions or even ignite wars. So vital are our names that we've made defamation a criminal act in many places. In some cultures, verbal offenses are seen as even more grievous than physical harm. Take the Chippewa Indians: while one tribe member can kill and eat another's totem animal, mocking that same animal brings severe punishment.[52] This fascinating custom reveals the immense power of words to shape reality and identity.

The Bible's Book of Revelation resonates with this idea, depicting Jesus as the Rider on the White Horse. A sword extends from his mouth 'to strike down nations' (Revelation 19:15), symbolizing the awe-inspiring power of the spoken word. This imagery underscores the unparalleled capacity of words, spoken, written, or thought, to shape our lives, identities, and the world we inhabit.

Words possess the singular power to deeply affect us, sending shivers down our spine or moving us to tears. Life-changing moments are often punctuated by expressions like 'I love you', which can transform our existence indefinitely. As we articulate these words, something within us shifts, and history is shaped by declarations like 'I have a dream' or philosophical insights such as 'I think, therefore I am'. Words, in many ways, become events that construct the framework for our existence.

Inhabiting a world of words, we dwell within a linguistic house. Our thoughts and interpretations are filtered through language, which animates our daily routines of reading the news, listening to podcasts, or watching TV. Without words, events would cease to exist, and the medium of language would dissolve, leaving the message of our being untold.

Imagine a football game devoid of commentary, a sensation of emptiness pervading the experience. Throughout history, humankind has yearned for explanations and narratives to comprehend the world. From religious tales to scientific theories, language has been our guiding star, illuminating the events and phenomena around us.

In our contemporary landscape, commentary is omnipresent: news, politics, religion, literature, and sports. Engaging with the news isn't solely about acquiring knowledge; often, we simply crave new words and the sensation of participating in the action. As the saying goes, 'Dog bites man, is not news. Man bites dog is news.' The Word, language, and commentary act as the lifeblood of our collective experience.

Engaging with the news or watching TV transports us to the heart of events, as Marshall McLuhan insightfully noted that people don't just read newspapers; they immerse themselves in them daily, akin to stepping into a hot bath. It's in this realm of words where the action truly unfolds, making us feel like attendees at a gathering.

'The Word ushers us into time...' Jacques Ellul observed, 'It makes us live with endless misunderstandings, interpretations, and overtones.'[53] Offering narratives to guide our lives endlessly, it is through these misunderstandings and diverse interpretations of essential, deep texts that our civilizations take shape. A deep thinker, claimed Nietzsche, dreads being understood more than being misunderstood.

We persistently delve into the meanings of words, seeking understanding and interpretation. Through language, we gossip, comment, criticize, lead, and follow. Dictators, wielding authoritarian words, dictating the scripts societies obey. Yet, no dictator could surpass the dictate of an ultimate mysterious authority: the origin of the Word. Is God responsible? Perhaps. Whatever it is, this authority possesses the last word, as it embodies the Word itself. Language, transcending our individual existences, guarantees the perpetual interpretation of discourse. Thus, human existence is characterized by an ongoing process of questioning and discussing.

In the beginning, the Word remained undefined, its meaning unuttered. This vagueness bears a profound message: to be is to speak and to seek. As long as we exist, we will employ the Word, but its definition and ultimate destination will stay enigmatic. As long as we live, we will share the Word, confessing it to one another.

To Exist Is to Confess

Therefore, confess your sins to one another and pray for one another, that you may be healed.

(James 5:16)

Existence unfolds as a story, a linguistic journey defining the very essence of our humanity. More than mere speech, it encompasses confession: not solely a religious act, but a vital expression of our shared human experience. Language demands our engagement, compelling us to voice our concerns, our truths. 'Language is neither reactionary nor progressive', Roland Barthes once said. 'It is quite simply fascist; for fascism does not prevent speech, it compels speech.'

Priests, psychologists, and psychiatrists serve as sounding boards for our confessions, allowing us to speak and bring our past into the present. As Steiner suggests, the task of psychoanalysis is to 'derive and give substantive authority to a verbal construct of the past'.[54] Films like *Shutter Island* illustrate the power of letting patients speak and act out their buried traumas, retrieving the core of who they truly are. In the movie, the innovative clinicians of Shutter Island stage an elaborate scene to help 'detective' Teddy Daniels (Leonardo DiCaprio) confront his self-deception, ultimately revealing that he himself is the missing patient he seeks. Our true nature often lies hidden, even from ourselves; by reenacting our own stories, we delve into the depths of our forgotten pasts and recover the essence of our being.

Expressing ourselves is both empowering and necessary, as Dostoevsky brilliantly captures in virtually all his works. In *The Gambler*, he highlights the importance of communication as a means of overcoming existential anxiety and alienation:

'I care not whether it be wise or stupid', I cried in return. 'I only know that in your presence I must speak, speak, speak. Therefore, I am speaking. I lose all conceit when I am with you, and everything ceases to matter.'[55]

Dostoevsky explores the human need for confession even more deeply in his groundbreaking novel *Crime and Punishment*. The story revolves around the protagonist, Rodion Raskolnikov, who decides to commit a heinous act, murder, believing he is above society's conventional morals. Inspired by historical figures like Napoleon, who Raskolnikov believes transcends human laws, he justifies his crime as an act of greatness by killing an unscrupulous pawnbroker.

However, after committing the crime, Raskolnikov is plagued by an unexpected and crushing guilt that weighs heavily on his conscience. His true punishment isn't the prospect of imprisonment but rather the unbearable burden of keeping his terrible secret. The inability to confess his crime turns Raskolnikov's existence into a living nightmare, filled with unbearable misery and torment.

The name 'Raskolnikov', derived from the Russian word *raskol*, meaning 'split' or 'schism', conveys a powerful message about the nature of confession. Raskolnikov's crime divides his personality, pitting his external persona against his inner self. This conflict becomes a metaphor for an existential crisis, emphasizing the importance of truth and confession in our lives. Through confession, we embrace our humanity and seek connection with others, transforming ourselves and the world around us.

Raskolnikov reaches a breaking point, unable to withstand his isolation from society any longer, and finally confesses his heinous crime. It turns out that even the prison sentence he faces is not as terrible as keeping the dreadful secret to himself: 'Why does my action strike them as so horrible?' he said to himself. 'Is it because it was a crime? What is meant by crime? My conscience is at rest. Of course, it was a legal crime, of course, the letter of the law was broken and blood was shed. Well, punish me for the letter of the law ... and that's enough.'[56] In the lines that follow, he acknowledges that his true crime is not murder but the inability to resist confessing. It was this that separated him from the great men of history, those who transcended all morals and laws, like Napoleon. 'Of course, in that case many of the benefactors of mankind who snatched power for themselves instead of inheriting it ought to have been punished at their first steps. But those men succeeded and so they were right, and I didn't, and so I had no right to have taken that step.' It was only in that that he recognized his criminality, only in the fact that he had been unsuccessful and had confessed it.

Recall the first rule of *Fight Club*? 'Do not talk about Fight Club.' The second rule? 'Do NOT talk about Fight Club.' All other rules, including the fighting and violence, paled in comparison to the fundamental rule: keeping Fight Club a secret until the very end. Like Raskolnikov's story, Fight Club is a tale of inner struggle, a physical fight with the protagonist's own alter ego (Tyler Durden); a complete split within one and the same person. The imaginary Fight Club begins to crumble as soon as the protagonist starts confessing. Once the first and most important rule of not speaking about Fight Club is broken, the illusory world of violence and inner struggle starts falling apart. The truth eventually emerges, and the darkness enveloping the internal fight club dissipates.

Raskolnikov's internal strife ultimately subsides when he confesses his crime to the outside world. He knew he needed to do so to alleviate his anguish. Had Raskolnikov possessed the strength to persevere in his deception, he would have triumphed and attained the 'greatness' he believed in. However, he fell short. Raskolnikov was not as exceptional as the historical figures he admired; rather, he was an ordinary man who prioritized life over grandeur. He longed to rejoin society and participate in the human condition.

In stark contrast to Raskolnikov is Dostoevsky's other protagonist: Prince Lev Nikolayevich Myshkin from *The Idiot*. Myshkin is considered an idiot because, unlike everyone around him, he is the most honest person one could ever meet. He has no secrets from anyone, and unlike Raskolnikov, who suffered greatly from being a walking secret, Myshkin is an open book. In any situation, Myshkin remains honest to the very end, astonishing everyone around him. His honesty quickly earns him admiration, respect, and even the affectionate love of the novel's most sought-after women.

Dostoevsky's Prince Myshkin, an exceptional character, exemplifies the ultimate 'positive and beautiful man'.[57] As a near-divine figure, his unyielding honesty reveals the significance of harmonizing our inner and outer worlds. Achieving this balance demands immense courage and integrity, making Myshkin a captivating outsider; indeed, an 'idiot'.

Much like Jesus, Myshkin stands as a luminous beacon of truth amidst a sea of deceit. In his literary masterpiece, Dostoevsky may have sought to embody the Greek concept of *Aletheia,* truth and unconcealment, through this character. Myshkin, a modern martyr, follows the legacy of Socrates and Jesus, known for their unwavering honesty.

When Diogenes the Cynic was asked why he was walking around in broad daylight with a lit lamp, he famously answered: 'I am looking for an honest man.' Truth has always been rare and even idiotic. It is always an exception, a gem hard to find even in broad daylight. 'What is spoken is never and in no language what is said', says Heidegger. Our inherent tendency to conceal ourselves behind words turns the pursuit of truth and its accurate expression into an almost celestial feat.

Politics, too, can benefit from its share of 'idiots'. In the public sphere, political leaders act as the mask society dons in order to express itself in the public arena. The politician becomes the public's primary spokesperson, amplifying the voice of the masses. Levi-Strauss notes that the public's dissatisfaction with politicians and leaders often stems from the simple fact that direct conversation is lacking. 'My relationship with the President of the Republic', he writes, 'consists exclusively in negative observances, since in the absence of other bonds our possible relations are entirely defined by the rule that I will not speak to him unless he invites me to do so, and that I will keep myself at a respectful distance from him.'[58] The public passively observes the political persona speaking on their behalf but rarely has the opportunity to engage with them in an active, face-to-face dialogue.

In the current era of heightened political correctness, which often involves concealing truth to avoid offending certain groups, the stakes for speaking the truth candidly have risen. Political correctness leads to hiding behind words and avoiding confession. This presents a significant dilemma in the Western political landscape today. Populist leaders frequently gain support based on their blunt and even offensive language, acting as the designated confessors of the public. These leaders, often seen as 'riders on the white horse', wield sharp words to cut through the concealment, attracting votes through their directness, openness, and perceived honesty.

In both politics and everyday life, comedians also act as indispensable 'idiots' who deftly navigate sensitive topics. They employ comedy and irony to express thoughts indirectly, thereby avoiding offense. The Greek term *eironeia*, meaning 'simulated ignorance', captures the essence of a comedian's approach, revealing the truth while shrouding it in humour. Comedy artfully uncovers the hidden while simultaneously veiling the obvious, allowing words to cleverly hide in plain sight.

As Thomas Mann observed, 'every confession is violence'. Thus, comedy serves as an essential and effective means of illuminating truth within the shadows of the unspoken. Legendary Soviet comedian Mikhail Zhvanetsky aptly remarked, 'a low quality of life nurtures a high quality of humour.' Comedy thrives as a coping mechanism in the face of harsh realities. In societies where truth is repressed, comedy must rise to the challenge of confronting such constraints. For Nietzsche, irony represented a sign of health, while absolutism belonged to the realm of pathology.

In the Age of the Internet and social media, we find ourselves immersed in an era of public confessions and storytelling. No longer do we confess anonymously in church or privately in diaries like Augustine's *Confessions*. In a secular world, our confessions have shifted from a vertical connection with God to a horizontal connection with one another. The decline in faith in the Western world seems to be closely linked to our insatiable desire to enhance communication technologies and share our stories with others. We now consume words more voraciously than products, craving inclusion in a narrative or the opportunity to share our own.

Our collective memories, stored digitally as 'data', have become a commodity more valuable than oil.[59] The digital age has transformed the logos, the word, into a high-priced asset. The focus of the technological age is not on technology itself, but on the logos and our embodied experience of the world, recalling that *digitus* in Latin means 'finger' and technology signifies the art of 'crafting the logos'.[60] The immense market capitalization of today's tech giants showcases the power of the word in the information age, which emphasizes talking about things rather than producing them. Recent advancements in AI based on the so-called LLMs (Large Language Models) is truly a matter of concern, since the entire tapestry of human existence is now at stake. As the French philosopher Paul Virilio noted: to invent the ship is to invent the shipwreck.

But the concept of the word as a commodity is not new. Christ's statement, 'people do not live by bread alone but by every word that comes from the mouth of God' (Matthew 4:4), alludes to the word as sustenance. Replacing 'the mouth of God' with technology ushers in a technological era where technology serves as our new church and the primary modern platform for confessions. We shall talk about this more in Part III.

The Voice of God

Since God creates through his Word, it creates everyone.

—Jacques Ellul

Religions around the world serve as the glue that binds us together (from the Latin *re-ligare*, meaning 'to bind'). They fulfil our innate human need to confess to a higher power, intertwining the concepts of confession and religion. As we communicate with the divine, we engage our inner voice, with God acting as both the listener and the conduit. The term 'god' originates from the Proto-Indo-European *ghut*, meaning 'to call' or 'to invoke'. In this way, God is both what is invoked and the one who invokes, becoming the very essence of ex-sistence: an emergence out of and into itself. By engaging this voice, we bring God's presence into the world, unveiling and creating *goodness*. Jewish folklore even wonders if God created humans to hear them tell tales,[61] suggesting that we are actors in the cosmic theatre of being, voicing God's words through our own.

In the Bible's Book of Revelation, it states, 'I am the Alpha and the Omega, the first and the last, the beginning and the end' (Revelation 22:13). This reference to the Greek alphabet's initial and final letters emphasizes that God has the first and last word, delivering the ultimate judgement. In Islam, the Quran ('recital') was dictated to the Prophet Mohammed by God's voice. Just as in Greek and Hebrew, the Arabic language highlights the connection between hearing and obeying God's voice, with 'Islam' meaning 'submission'.

The three Abrahamic faiths, Christianity, Judaism, and Islam, each approach God's voice differently. Christianity uniquely incarnates God's voice through Jesus Christ, whereas Islam and Judaism avoid personifying God. Islam strictly forbids any depiction of a personified God, while Judaism prohibits writing

God's full name. Instead, the Tetragrammaton (YHWH) is used, concealing God's full name, Yahweh. By not reducing God to a single entity like Christianity, Islam and Judaism preserve the divine as an unpersonified voice, honouring the transcendent nature of the divine.

In Christianity, the Word becomes flesh in the form of Jesus, the personified incarnation of the divine. This personification might have led to a diminished emphasis on the Word's importance, overshadowing the voice of God Himself. Steiner observes that Judaism, unlike Christianity, lacks a specific time and place for creation and keeps the Messiah's coming open-ended.[62] By personifying God as Jesus, Christianity shifted from a religious focus to a historiographical one. However, history, based on investigation,[63] risks nullifying itself when it identifies the subject as a mere individual instead of a god. This distinction between religion, founded on faith, and history, based on knowledge, highlights a potential weakness in Christianity's treatment of the Word. As faith in Jesus waned, Christianity faced a crisis that edged toward nihilism. Did the Christian doctrine of incarnation lay the groundwork for its own existential struggle?

Dostoevsky, deeply devout, recognized the vulnerability within Christianity's tendency to personify the divine. He understood that defining God as a specific individual, even Jesus, risked reducing the divine to a mere historical figure; a person, but not the essence of the faith. In *The Grand Inquisitor*, he argues that God's truth transcends any individual, even if that individual is the very foundation of the faith.

The Grand Inquisitor's message to Christ is clear: all human acts are carried out in his name, but the actual persona must recede into the background. For Dostoevsky, God is not Jesus, but the timeless, mythical narrative: 'We are not with you but with *Him*.' The human voice seeks the unnamed father, not the incarnated 'Son of God', emphasizing the importance of the

Word and the voice over mere personification and idolatry. This focus on the essence of faith, rather than the figurehead, illustrates Dostoevsky's deep understanding of the transcendent nature of the divine.

Language plays a critical role in this discussion, as it is the foundation for our belief in the Word. We don't merely possess knowledge about language; we have trust and unquestionable faith in it. This faith in language is so vital that the potential crisis within Christianity isn't solely about belief in God, but also, and more importantly, the belief in the logos itself.

Messengers of the Gods

Inspire me, O gods (it is you who
have even
transformed my art), and spin me a thread
from the world's beginning
down to my own lifetime, in one continuous
poem.

—Ovid

Religious stories serve as binding meta-narratives that lend meaning to our languages. We learn our first languages through stories, making sense of words by associating them with a broader context. Stories offer a framework, connecting individual words and sentences to a larger whole. They shape our value systems, distinguishing between good and evil, courage and cowardice, and the divine and the mundane. Wittgenstein noted that language functions as a game of associations (*Sprachspiel*), whereby a word can only be understood within a sentence, and 'to understand a sentence means to understand a language'.[64] Every part is always related to the whole, and the whole to its parts.

Sacred stories form the foundation of our cultures, arising organically like language itself. They provide immediate context for our understanding of the world. And what context can there be without an actual text? Without the Bible, there would be no Western culture as we know it. Similarly, the Bible owes its existence to the ancient Greek epics, such as Homer's *Odyssey* and *Iliad*, which inspired later narratives.

Many modern words derive from ancient myths, epics, and poems. For instance, 'echo' comes from the name of a mountain nymph in Greek mythology, 'sirene' from the sea nymphs who attempted to seduce Odysseus, and 'cloth' from Clotho, the youngest of the Three Fates. Even the name of a continent, Europa, stems from a mythological figure: the Phoenician princess abducted by Zeus in the guise of a bull.

Ancient Greek, a language foundational to European tongues, was preserved and passed down through the epic poems of Homer and Hesiod. Eric Havelock, in his book *Preface to Plato*, argues that these epics served not just artistic and cultural purposes but also fulfilled practical needs in daily life. Early Greeks who could not read or write had to rely on memorizing these stories in rhyme, weaving together law, literature, customs, etiquette, and values into an oral document.[65]

Recitation sustained both the narrative and language, while shared tales and value systems united the Greeks, solidifying their social fabric. Plato even dubbed Homer the 'prime educator of Greece', acknowledging the crucial role his poems played in shaping society. This unity gave rise to a singular culture and the persona as the protagonist in theatre, underlining the potency of language and storytelling in defining human identity and experience. Intriguingly, the theory of human nature emerged from the theatre itself, both words sharing the Greek root *thea*, denoting 'view' or 'spectacle'. A persona's actions are dictated by theatre, by acting out stories.

Greek poets and minstrels sustained stories through their remarkable memory and eloquence. In those early times, poetry was vital for self-understanding and for connecting with others in the culture. The term *poiesis* in ancient Greek simply meant 'to create', encompassing not only the crafting of poems or verses, but any act or process of creation.

In his masterwork, *Poetics*, Aristotle calls the poet 'the maker', highlighting the origin of poetry in our deeply human instinct for imitating nature through the power of words. The poet becomes the messenger of nature, the messenger of the gods. By mirroring nature with his words, the poet brings it into the realm of human experience and reality. He or she lays the foundations of our great meta-stories by expanding our linguistic world and, consequently, our being in it. The poet is the master of metaphor, adept at translating the language of nature into something we can understand and interpret through human language.

Aristotle provides an example of how a poet creates new ways of seeing things by simply giving them a name: 'For instance, to scatter seed is called sowing: but the action of the sun in scattering his rays is nameless. Still, this process bears to the sun the same relation as sowing to the seed. Hence the expression of the poet "sowing the god-created light".'[66] The poet metaphorically names a natural phenomenon, bringing awareness to something that was previously unnamed. As Rilke asks, 'How can fingers point out a smell?'

Indeed, can we not say that the poet is the most original thinker? As posed by Nietzsche, 'What is originality? It is to see something that as yet has no name, that cannot be referred to, even though it is hiding in plain sight. Men as they usually are require a name for a thing before it is visible to them at all. For the most part, those with originality have also been those who gave things their names.'[67] The poet is the one who makes something exist: the original being occurs in the logos. Originality implies origins, and the origin of all things, physical or abstract, lies nowhere else but in the word.

The act of speaking is an act of creation, of poetry. No word in our language escapes metaphor or poetic essence. When silence shatters, pierced by our utterance, poetic creation emerges: something born from nothing, a manifestation of *ex-sistence*; of being and truth. As Bachelard says, 'A poet's word, because it strikes true, moves the very depths of our being.'[68] Truth, akin to language, is not contrived or calculated; it simply is.

In German and Dutch, *Dichter* denotes a poet, its essence subtly drawn from the Latin *dictare*, suggesting the act of speaking or dictating. Thus, the poet is 'the speaker', the foremost among all, even the chief dictator. But what is it that the poet dictates? They speak of nothing specific, yet encompass everything.

While their words may lack immediate practical utility, they convey what is most essential to human nature, being, establishing the poet as its primary emissary. Much like nature, the poet's words hide in plain sight, concealing their core message. Yet, attentive listening unveils more than first perceived. Through poetry, one discovers the truth of existence.

In Rilke's poetic words:

You are lonely, my friend, because you are...
We, with a word or a finger-sign,
gradually make the world our own.

The Language Where Languages End

The country known to me, to whose furthest boundaries I intend to go in order to discover music, is language.

—Kierkegaard

What is music to the human being? It is not just sound, noise, or mere vibrations in the air. While these elements exist in nature, the beauty of music lies in its existence solely in the human ear.

Animals can hear sounds and noises, but they cannot perceive the orderly rhythm of music as we do. If human ears did not exist, neither would music. Perhaps, without music, there would be no human beings either.

When humans dance to music, they become a complete persona, as the sound of music courses through their entire body down to the last fingertip. Perhaps we are even more of a persona when we dance than when we do not. In dance, we become music. Nietzsche once said that he could only believe in a god who could dance, and he understood the profound significance of that statement.

Music is unique because it is more than mere sound, even patterned sound that some animals and birds have been known to react to in a dance-like manner. To equate music with mere sound would be to misunderstand its essence entirely. Music is order and meaning. It evokes happiness, joy, melancholy, nostalgia, energy, and so much more. Music gives us a certain disposition, it positions us within itself, and in it being manifests itself in profound and mysterious ways. It always carries a message without ever saying anything concrete. Rilke beautifully described music as the 'language where languages end'. Music, the sister of language, may be the closest manifestation of our existential or even *ex-static* relationship with the symphony of being. It is external to us, yet we feel it as an inseparable part of ourselves. 'To ask "what is music?"' says Steiner, 'may well be one way of asking "what is man?"'[69]

In Plato's *Republic*, music held such significance that it was taught as a science, on par with mathematics and geometry. Plato observed that music infiltrated the soul, shaping our sense of beauty and deformity, first unconsciously, then consciously as reason emerged.[70] As a friend of being, music may be the most potent expression of a religious experience, especially in our secular times. Nowadays, it is not the priest but the rock star in a concert or the DJ in a club who unites souls in ecstatic presence. Music is spaceless yet places everyone in the same place we call rhythm, a common invisible truth.

Language and music share close ties, potentially with identical origins. Humboldt posited that humans are singing creatures, and every language has its melody.[71] This melodic essence is evident in children acquiring accents before language,[72] as well as learners grasping a new language's melody before its vocabulary. Some languages even feature unique communication forms closer to music than simple speech, such as African drum languages and the Canary Islands' 'Silbo Gomero', a form of whistled Spanish. Words are indeed music to our ears.

Poems, our first songs, and words, our first instruments, embody the musical element. Jazz, a language in itself, stems from the French *jaser*, meaning 'to chatter', reflecting human conversation's spontaneous, improvisational nature. Listening to the unpredictable jazzy rhythm, we can imagine ourselves in a bustling tavern in Louisiana or a lively bar in New York City with pleasant chatter all around. Music transcends linguistic barriers, providing a universal language that harmonizes disparate cultures and nationalities, as evident in Stefan Zweig's testimony of nineteenth-century Vienna: 'For the genius of Vienna — a specifically musical one — was always that it harmonized all the national and lingual contrasts.'[73] Could music be the solution to the Tower of Babel?

Music, like being, relies on memory, harmonizing past, present, and future. Our brains, natural time machines, synchronize musical sounds and tones, creating harmony within the being called music. Time, the concern of all concerns, is inextricably linked to memory, music, and being. As Rilke observed, 'Song is existence.'

In our quest to understand the enigma of being, music offers a clearer insight into the orderly yet hidden structure. Listening to a piece of music, we hear several notes at once, understanding the melody's flow and how it evolves over time. Music allows us to exist simultaneously in the past, present, and future, achieving the most harmonious order. Mann's Lodovico Settembrini in *The Magic Mountain* says, 'Music awakens time, awakens us to our finest enjoyment of time.' Music grants time its primary means of expression, with our brain functioning like an orchestra conductor, synchronizing scattered musical sounds and tones. Like the conductor, we ensure harmony within the symphony of existence we call music. A symphony is a joining of sounds in time; symphonizing means synchronizing. Just as music is a manifestation and expression of being, so is time itself.

This connection leads us to another kindred soul of memory, music, and being as a whole: time. Concern, the fundamental trait that makes humans who they are, renders everything real in the human world, and time is at the top of our hierarchy of concerns. It is no surprise that 'time' is the most used noun in the English language, alongside the most used verb, 'to be'. The connection between the two will be explored in the next part.

Part II Where Is Time?

In Search of Lost Time

For he learns to understand the expression 'It was,' that password with which struggle, suffering, and weariness come over human beings, so as to remind him what his existence basically is — a never completed past tense.

—Nietzsche

We seek not the present but the past, not joy, for that is always present, but sorrow, because its nature is to pass by.

—Kierkegaard

In Christopher Nolan's film, the protagonist wields a single word, 'Tenet', as his tool to thwart an impending cataclysm. Tasked with navigating time in reverse, he confronts nature's laws to fulfil his objective. The word 'Tenet' itself is the secret: it remains unchanged, whether read forwards or backwards.

Nolan illuminates the enigmatic interplay between present and past, between progressive and regressive motion. Time is indeed an enigma. We seem to move through time, rewinding and fast-forwarding as if it were a straightforward path. We base our financial forecasts, personal plans, and socio-political systems on this linear metaphor of time moving 'forward'. However, our experiences reveal a more intricate nature. Time is erratic, advancing in unpredictable ways. The past, though no longer present, still impacts our lives. The future never really comes, but we await it with each passing moment. The present vanishes the moment we notice it. Time, like being itself, evades clear definition and comprehension, it hides in plain sight in the most interesting ways. Sartre's Roquentin, in *Nausea*, captures the dilemma: 'I wanted the moments of my life to follow each other, lining up in order, like the moments of the life that you remember. But this is like trying to catch time by the tail.'

Time's primary challenge is its elusive quality. It isn't linear or sequential. Time seems to be nothing, yet it encompasses everything. Our memory turns time into a series of consecutive events, crafting a logical, orderly story. In the end, time is a compilation of moments sewn together by our memory, forming a metaphorical journey. We exist in the present, experiencing one moment at a time, but it's our recollection of the past that provides our experience of time with coherence and order. This puzzling nature of time links to the essence of being, truth, and memory, exposing a deep interconnection between these ideas that continue to shape our understanding of the world and ourselves.

The Russian word for time, *vremya*, shares roots with *vertet*, meaning 'to turn'. Insightful, as time doesn't march in a straight line, but spins, returns, and circles. The universe, a cosmic sway of time's rotations (*uni-vertere*: 'one turn' in Latin). Time's origin? Ourselves.

Numerous accounts of near-death experiences repeatedly convey the same idea: that one's entire life flashes before their eyes in an instant right before death. In that final moment, it seems as if the whole of one's past being is revealed in a feedback loop. Neuroscientist Dean Buonomano provides an account of this phenomenon, citing Swiss geologist Albert Heim's 1892 study of near-death experiences among members of the Swiss Alpine Club. Heim's findings emphasize the 'dominant mental quickness and sense of surety' experienced during these events, as well as the sensation of time expanding.[1]

Dostoevsky, who himself had many near-death experiences due to epilepsy, offers a powerful description of the mysterious nature of time through the character of Prince Myshkin. Myshkin explains that every moment of time is a lifetime of its own, and in the final moments of life, our past returns to us in unimaginable ways. 'These (near-death) instants were characterized — to define it in a word — by an intense quickening of the sense of personality. Since, in the last conscious moment preceding the attack, he could say to himself, with full understanding of his words: "I would give my whole life for this one instant", then doubtless to him it really was worth a lifetime. [...] "I feel then as if I understood those amazing words — There shall be no more time."' Memory connects each instant, but each moment is a world apart. Bachelard, in his *Intuition of the Instant*, says: 'When that shattering instant arrives as the eyes of a cherished being close forever, we immediately feel the hostile novelty of the next instant that comes to pierce the heart.'[2] All of being is compressed in time, the primary measurement of which is the instant: the heartbeat of time.

But what is happening with time? Is it moving forward as we traditionally understand it, or backward toward the memory of the past? Our experience suggests the latter. Ex-pereo signifies a backward-looking journey, not a forward one. Aristotle posits that one cannot remember the present, only the past.[3] In essence, time does not move forward into 'what will be', but instead moves backward through memory into 'what was'. As soon as we utter the words 'I am' or 'it is', time has already passed, and we have experienced a being that is no more, only to return to it through our memory. It consumes everything we say or think, but through language, we can retrieve it from the already bygone past. This is where language plays a crucial role, and more importantly, where human concern manifests itself to the fullest. Thanks to language, memory, and concern, what was in the past remains present.

Steiner emphasizes the duality of language and time, explaining that language occurs in time and every speech act literally 'takes time', as the common expression goes.[4] Language shares with time the sensation of the irreversible, moving away from us in the moment it is realized. As we think or speak, time passes and cannot be reversed. The moment I say 'now', it has already disappeared and is no longer now; it merely 'took time'.

But even though language takes time away from us, it provides us with words, meanings, memory, and experience. Language bestows us with being by giving us something instead of nothing, and the price we pay for this is time.

We converse not of the future but of the past. Although we may sense forward motion as we think or speak, our ultimate destination is consistently the past. McLuhan's metaphor of driving the car of time forward while gazing only at the rear-view mirror aptly captures this notion. As he posits, we perpetually 'march backward into the future'.

As our eyes glide across the text, a curious phenomenon unfolds. Sentences blossom into comprehension only upon reaching their terminus: the full stop. Yet, as we traverse the linear expanse, our genuine understanding of each word and phrase gallops in reverse: back through the winding paths of language. This dance applies to single sentences, conglomerates of clauses, and even language in its entirety.

Consider this anecdote: 'In my childhood, I excelled in class, earning admiration from all. I emerged victorious in every sports competition I joined. Yet, none of this is true.' The reader may experience frustration or betrayal for taking their time to read a series of sentences that happened to be not true at the end. Fortunately, language harbours safeguards against frivolous wordplay, for time is a treasure not to be frittered away. The Bible itself warns of reckoning for idle chatter: 'But I tell you that everyone will have to give account on the day of judgement for every empty word they have spoken' (Matthew 12:36). Language whispers, urging us toward more profound, more captivating exchanges. Indeed, Ovid's *Metamorphoses* recounts how the raven's talkative nature and blithe tongue transformed its pristine white plumage into an inky black: 'His tongue was the cause of the raven's downfall; thanks to his talkative nature, his earlier whiteness of colour was changed to its opposite.'

While reading, we navigate through the ocean of time, questing for truth, only to be yanked back into the depths of the past. The final flourish of a sentence can negate all that preceded it, unveiling the ultimate truth. Each new word and phrase illuminates its predecessors, all unfolding in a mysterious dance of retrospection.

In certain languages, verbs linger at the sentence's end, withholding meaning until their revelation. In German and Dutch, one proclaims, 'I will the book read', rather than, 'I will read the book.' Until encountering the verb 'read' at the finale, the sentence's essence remains unclear. Buonomano offers two simple examples: 'the mouse broke' versus 'the mouse died'.[5] The sentence's conclusion shapes its inception, and the verb determines the noun. Our perception of the past as 'left' and the future as 'right' is deeply rooted in culture and language, intricately woven into how we read and write.

In Hebrew[6] and Aymara, conceptions of past and future deviate from English norms. For instance, in Aymara, the word for past signifies 'eyes' or 'sight', while the word for future translates to 'back' or 'behind'. With the past unfurling before them and the future trailing behind, they appear to stride backward into the future.

Notions of 'forward' and 'backward' vary across languages, inviting the possibility that 'forward' could be just a camouflaged misspelling of 'foreword'. Steiner, for instance, cites Petrarch, who in his 1338 work *Africa*, inverts the time-axis, urging the young to 'walk back into the pure radiance of the past', as the classic past embodies the true future.[7]

Might the past be our rightful future? For Homer's Odysseus, his past (the return to Ithaca) served as his future destination, and Dante condemned soothsayers and fortune-tellers in Hell by twisting their heads backward. The past offers invaluable lessons for the future, yet we can only gaze upon the past, while the future remains cloaked in obscurity. After all, in life's final moments, one's existence often 'flashes back' rather than 'forward'.

Everything we see, including light, is always a few nanoseconds in the past, as it takes time to reach our eyes and brains. A falling star, for example, may have already fallen years ago, but we perceive it in the present due to the time it takes light to travel across the universe. This creates a unique phenomenon where we see in the present what has happened in the past but no longer exists in time or space, existing only in our memory.

Romanian poet Mihai Eminescu illustrates this enigmatic phenomenon in his poem *For the Star*:

It's been a long way for that star
Now rising in our skies:
Its light has trekked a thousand years
To reach our earthborn eyes.
It may have long ago burned out
Amid the blue of space
Yet only now its ray has come
To set our sights ablaze.[8]

Our perception of sound and music also reflects this notion. When we first hear a favourite song, we may not realize we like it until we listen to it again. This repetition and familiarity provide comfort and a sense of a temporal home.

Repetition is, therefore, an essential aspect of music, making it harmonious by nature, and contributes to the harmony of our existence through the turning and returning of time. In this context, we can understand the story of language and our being through the lens of music. 'The ideal', wrote Cioran, 'is to be able to repeat oneself like... Bach.'[9]

Homer's tale of Odysseus weaves a tapestry illustrating the quest for the past amidst an unfamiliar and hostile present. Bearing the name 'Son of Pain',[10] Odysseus embodies nostalgia, a Greek notion signifying 'returning home in pain'. This odyssey of nostalgia resonates within each of us, as we embark on our own voyage of seeking lost time.

As we traverse the ever-shifting terrain of time, language, and memory, our lives intertwine with the intricate connections between past, present, and future. The present, a fleeting moment, is inevitably shaped by the echoes of our past experiences. Steve Jobs, in his poignant Stanford commencement speech, posits that connecting life's dots is achievable only in hindsight.[11] Placing faith in our instincts, destiny, life, or karma, Jobs says, we trust that these dots will ultimately coalesce into a meaningful future.

Jobs was an ambitious visionary. But contrary to popular belief, ambition transcends a linear path forward. Rather, it frequently involves a spiral journey, circling back to confront and surmount past fears and challenges, ultimately leading to self-discovery. *Ambitio*, meaning 'going round in circles', underscores the cyclical nature of ambition, emphasizing the crucial role of memory and self-reflection in personal growth and success.

In Mann's *The Magic Mountain*, the manner in which our memories of the past continuously resurface in our present is masterfully depicted. Love, naturally, plays a central role. The novel recounts an odd event in which memory and time play tricks on protagonist Hans Castorp as he encounters the Russian lady Clavdia Chauchat at a Swiss sanatorium and falls in love with her. Strangely, his feelings are triggered by her resemblance to a boy named Pribislav Hippe, whom he met in primary school but never saw again. Castorp's infatuation with Chauchat begins at an odd moment: when he asks her for a pencil. This seemingly mundane event mirrors precisely how Castorp met Hippe, too. Two memorable yet seemingly disconnected events collide, and Castorp finds himself suddenly smitten by love.

This fascinating interplay between the past and present selves mirrors the wandering paths of Nietzsche's prophet Zarathustra and Homer's adventurous Odysseus, who eventually return to their past. Zarathustra's restlessness, like Odysseus's, prevents him from staying in one place for long. Ultimately, one experiences only oneself, says Zarathustra, 'and what could fall to me now that is not already my own? It merely returns, it finally comes home to me — my own self and everything in it that has long been abroad and scattered among all things and accidents'.[12]

Zarathustra teaches the three metamorphoses in one's life: 'how the spirit becomes a camel, and the camel a lion, and finally the lion a child'. Zarathustra poses a question to his brothers: 'Why must the preying lion still become a child?' The answer lies in the fact that the child represents innocence, forgetting and a new beginning. The child, unlike the lion, is capable of embracing the game of creation, which requires a 'sacred yes-saying'. The film *The Curious Case of Benjamin Button* mirrors our shared experiences with Zarathustra, as we too journey through the complexities of time and memory back into childhood.

Nietzsche is not alone in his admiration for the wisdom and innocence of children; Kierkegaard also preferred talking with children: 'with them, one can still hope they may become rational beings; but those who have become that — Lord save us!'[13] Hans Christian Andersen, Kierkegaard's Danish compatriot, demonstrates the power of the child's perspective in his famous folktale *The Emperor's New Clothes*. The child hero is the only one who dares to proclaim the king's nakedness when all the adults pretend otherwise, compelled by public opinion and a fear of dissent. The child's honesty and disregard for societal norms unveil the truth that everyone else is unwilling to acknowledge.

Indeed, Fyodor Dostoevsky's *Idiot* Prince Myshkin, drawn to the company of children rather than adults, exemplifies the value of childlike qualities, such as honesty and authenticity, amidst a world of deception and pretence.

The connection between the Latin word *liberi*, meaning children, and the concept of liberty highlights the intrinsic intellectual freedom and even courage that children possess. Unencumbered by societal norms and expectations, children have the ability to see, question and express the world in its purest form.

Our journey through life is, in many ways, a struggle to recapture the innocence and freedom of childhood. By casting off the constraints imposed upon us by life and maturity, we can embrace the sacred yes-saying described by Zarathustra. This sentiment is echoed in the Gospel of Matthew (11:25), where Jesus praises the Father for revealing hidden truths to little children rather than the wise and learned.

Ultimately, our odyssey through time, language, and memory leads us to a deeper understanding of ourselves, our place in the world, and the profound wisdom that can be found in embracing the child within.

The Mysteries of the Future

Tomorrow, and tomorrow, and tomorrow,
Creeps in this petty pace from day to day,
To the last syllable of recorded time.

—Shakespeare, *Macbeth*

I stand, waiting for the future to embrace me. It approaches, unfailingly so. A moment more, and it shall become one with me. Yet, the future's rhythm is one of mystery; it arrives both always and never. As time's cadence unfolds, we find ourselves perpetually arriving somewhere. Yet, when the future's curtain falls, the present stage remains steadfast.

The future, an elusive phantom, forever dangles beyond our grasp. In its pursuit, we are like the ancient Elysian initiates, the *mysterion*, blindfolded to unveil the hidden mysteries. History's seers are often blind: Tiresias, Baba Vanga, even the Owl of Athena perched on her sightless side.[14] Like Beethoven, deaf composer of great symphonies, the blind are deemed the deepest visionaries. In the words of Heraclitus, 'Whoever cannot seek the unforeseen sees nothing, for the known way is an impasse.'

Yet, our beings are entwined with the future, woven into the fabric of our plans, predictions, and goals. We are, by nature, navigators of the yet-to-be. As we traverse time's labyrinth, seeking the future, we circle endlessly. For when the future is reached, it ceases to be; we remain in the present, the past as our compass. 'The future is stationary', Rilke writes to young poet Kappus, 'it is we who are moving in infinite space.'[15] In this expanse, we waltz with the memories of our past, rearranging and reflecting, attempting to decipher the future's enigmatic script.

The future, ever unpredictable, eludes our grasp, echoing Solon's wisdom to King Croesus: do not count on happiness until the end is known. In our quest to unveil the future's secrets, we find ourselves entwined in the tapestry of the past, as we seek meaning in the interplay of time.

The future, akin to the past, is a projection born from the present. Roquentin envisions the future as a shadowy mirage, scarcely discernible from the here and now.

'I see the future. It is there, poised over the street, hardly more dim than the present. What advantage will accrue from its realization?'[16] he muses. Our perception of time blurs, unable to disentangle the threads of present and future. We are driven to uncover the enigmatic future while tethered to the memory-laden past.

Like a spider plunging into the abyss while anchored to its web, Kierkegaard describes our venture into the future. Propelled by the past's momentum, we confront a life that is 'back-to-front and terrible, unendurable'.[17] Our ceaseless pursuit of the future arises from a yearning for security, for the unknown breeds fear. In Latin, *Sine cura* denotes 'without care', but can we truly be carefree as we face the unpredictable future? In our attempts to foresee and dominate the unknown, we seek solace from the uncertainty it begets. *Sine cura*, then, begets *curiosum*: carefulness, curiosity.

Curiosity about the future, at its core, emerges from our need for security. As Kahneman posits, 'survival prospects are poor for an animal that is not suspicious of novelty.'[18] Yet, if we shunned the veiled and the covered, our world would remain undiscovered. Thus, we brave the unknown, spurred by our insatiable curiosity and the primal instinct to survive.

This curiosity has led us to revere prophets, who are believed to possess knowledge of the future, shielding us from unforeseen calamities. Intriguingly, our most revered prophets, such as Jesus and Mohammed, hail from the past rather than the future. We turn to these ancient figures for guidance about the future, despite their teachings and writings originating millennia ago.

This paradox mirrors the cyclical essence of our existence, wherein everything in the universe appears to loop into and around itself. The Bible aptly states, 'What has been will be again, what has been done will be done again; there is nothing new under the sun' (Ecclesiastes 1:9). The enigma of the future relentlessly fascinates and tests us as we seek comprehension and solace in a world perpetually in flux.

The universe, a ceaseless cycle, revolves endlessly, returning to its genesis. Consequently, universal history might be a pattern that eternally recurs, embedded deeply within human nature.

Language plays a pivotal role in deciphering these cycles. Our sense of security largely resides in commentary and words, explaining why prophets have historically been entrusted with foretelling the future. However, can prediction exist without diction? The Greek term 'prophet' (*prophetes*) translates to 'spokesman'. Perhaps only God, embodying the totality of language, the alpha and the omega, can fully assume the prophetic mantle. Mortals, by comparison, are limited. Augustine cautions that the art of predicting the future is illusory, with human conjectures occasionally succeeding by mere chance.[19] As the adage goes, a broken clock is still accurate twice a day. We discuss the future so extensively that sometimes, we inadvertently stumble upon the truth. Steiner aptly observes that in German, those who 'promise' (*versprechen*) are also those who 'stumble over words' (*versprecher*).[20]

We ought to be cautious not just of others' prophecies but also of our own predictions. Frequently, we are unable to foresee our own words before they escape our lips. Consider moments when a sentence unexpectedly veers from its intended path, culminating in a manner entirely distinct from our original intention. In such instances, are we speaking, or is language speaking through us? McLuhan, a man of no small mental capability, concedes, 'I don't necessarily agree with everything I say.' If we always knew what we would say next, the world would unquestionably be more peaceful and harmonious. But while thinking before speaking appears ideal in theory, it is unfeasible in practice.

Our ignorance of the future renders life an exploration, and we traverse this journey by conversing with one another. However, as talking 'takes time', can we genuinely discuss the time consumed during our conversations? What remains to be spoken about if the subject of our discussion vanishes as we proceed? Are we merely pursuing shadows?

In the end, we employ language to mitigate the discomfort of the future's unpredictability. Our security lies in words, so our anxiety about facing the unknown future demands an expressive outlet: communication. Luhmann suggests 'that the future is unknowable is expressed in the present as communication. Society is irritated but has only one way to react to its irritation, in its own manner of operations: communication'.[21] Society responds to its irritation by talking, yet, since the events we discuss always precede our conversations about them, society remains one step behind, continuously agitated by the passage of time. Ironically, society tries to remedy this problem by consuming even more time in conversation. Ultimately, we find ourselves anchored in the same spot, as even revolutions, as the term implies, *revolve* around themselves in a circle of time.

To predict how a human might react to events, one would gain insights from studying the universal, unchanging aspects of humanity throughout history. Who better understands human nature than the poet: the master of language and the messenger of the gods?

For Aristotle, poetry, not history, provided a superior account of retelling the past and, therefore, the future. He believed that great poetry is an account of events that may recur, making it universal. In contrast, history is an incomplete account of specific events, limited to a particular time and place.[22] Aristotle questions the value of such trivial accounts. Don't we already spend too much time recounting stories that have no bearing on the future? We constantly seek universality: a pattern. When Tolstoy wrote *War and Peace*, he deliberately distorted historical dates and facts to create the narrative he wanted history to remember.[23] *War and Peace* is not a work of history but a work of art. Uninterpreted and disconnected facts serve no purpose in human history. A great work of fiction like *War and Peace* is more valuable to humanity than a mere collection of rigid, unrelated historical facts because people live within stories. A good story always reveals something about the universality of human nature. Father Time is called like that for a reason: it is linked to the Latin word for 'father' (*Pater*), suggesting pattern. We search for an orderly, understandable pattern in all human history, and we even revere this pattern.

Heidegger agrees with Aristotle, placing the poet above the historian. He saw the German Romantic poet Friedrich Hölderlin, whom he greatly admired, not as a messenger of the past but of the future. According to Heidegger, Hölderlin's verse was so exceptional, eternal, and universal that it could recur throughout human history. He writes, 'The precursor (Hölderlin) does not go off into a future; rather, he arrives out of that future, in such a way that the future is present only in the arrival of his words. The more purely the arrival happens, the more its remaining occurs as present.'[24]

The future is not a destination we reach by walking; time is not a literal road or journey but a metaphor. The future is continuously beneath our feet as we navigate the present, speak, and recall the past through our memories.

The question then arises: how do we cope with the unsettling unpredictability of the future? It appears that embracing it is the only option. The unknown future is essential and even desirable for human existence. Not knowing the future compels us to communicate and embark on a collective quest for truth. Luhmann posits that 'ignorance becomes the most important resource of action'.[25] If we knew everything about the future, we would not engage in conversation or action. For Luhmann, democracy entails not certainty but rather uncertainty about the future and the ultimate 'good'.

In contrast to autocracies and dictatorships, which claim to 'know' what is good for their societies, democracies operate differently. Democracies would not have functioning legal courts, free press, or nail-biting election nights if they knew in advance what is good for every citizen. In a genuine republic, everything is unpredictable, even contradictory, like time itself, because everyone participates in the discussion. In politics and life, ignorance is not a curse but a necessary evil.

Knowing the future in advance could be disastrous for life. Tolstoy argues that if we concede that human life can be governed by reason, the possibility of life itself is destroyed. Why engage in action if we already know the outcome? If that were the case, we would overthink everything before taking any action. If decisions could be predicted through rational thought, there would be no point in taking risks but only endless thinking. However, life requires us to make decisions, which inevitably involve risks and potential mistakes. The Greeks were well aware of this, as evidenced by their word for 'decision': *krisis*.

Conversely, if we knew all our actions in advance, we would become so bored with predictable outcomes that we would seek the unknown. Why engage in action if you know the result beforehand? What would be the purpose, excitement, and challenge of acting or even living life in general? The ancients were wise to view nature as a veiled goddess. Uncertainty and the mystery of human existence are necessary to cope with life. Otherwise, we would still be prone to searching for trouble simply because it is unpredictable and exciting. Dostoevsky states, 'Since man cannot live without miracles, he will provide himself with miracles of his own making. He will believe in witchcraft and sorcery, even though he may otherwise be a heretic, an atheist, and a rebel.'[26]

Living means acting blindfolded throughout life. Human existence is a mysterious, frightening, and often painful odyssey we all undertake until its inevitable end (the final outcome of which we already know, by the way). Not knowing the truth about the future is terrifying, but what is even scarier is knowing the truth about that very same future.

Just as the white raven turned black for talking too much, Ovid also shares the cautionary tale of Ocyrhoe, a water-nymph punished by the gods for her incessant prophecies about the future. As a symbol of her impatience, Ocyrhoe (meaning 'speed and mobility') was transformed into a swift horse. Hold your horses! said the angered gods:

> More words of fate remained to be spoken; but
> breathing a sigh
> from the depths of her heart, and bedewing her
> cheeks with a fountain of tears,
> the maiden continued: 'My destiny's running too
> fast, and I may not
> prophesy further. My powers of speech are being
> obstructed.
> My arts were purchased too dearly
> if they have directed the anger
> of heaven against me.
> I wish I had never foreknown the future!

A similar message emerges in Sophocles' *Oedipus Rex*. But this time, not about the future, but the past. King Oedipus' insatiable curiosity led him to seek too much knowledge about his past. The gods in the temple of Apollo foretold that he would kill his father and marry his mother. Despite his efforts to escape this fate, Oedipus unwittingly fulfilled the prophecy. When his relentless inquiries finally revealed the tragic and disgraceful truth, Oedipus blinded himself as punishment. Symbolic blindness here, once again, represents profound vision, for Oedipus saw too much and had to become blind (the Greek word *oida* means 'to know' or 'to have seen').

While Odysseus endures the pain of time by journeying backward through it, Oedipus sees through it, *inwards*, demonstrating the potential perils of knowing too much about one's past.

The lesson resonates: if we fast-forward or rewind through the song of existence, we miss the music that gives life its beauty. The ideal moment to tune into the symphony of being is always now: the present.

Now Is the Time

Therefore do not worry about tomorrow, for tomorrow will worry about itself.

(Matthew 6:34)

In investigating his deepest past, Oedipus uncovers a horrifying truth about his present situation. He learns that he is both the murderer of his father and the husband of his own mother, embodying the infamous Oedipal complex. Sophocles' tragedy conveys another message about time: we explore our past to understand who we are now. Paradoxically, it is not the past or the future that eludes us but the present itself. The present is the enigma to be unravelled, for it is the only moment that truly exists.

If human existence is a representation of time, it can only exist in the present. Contrary to popular belief, the past does not shape the present; rather, the present determines the past through memory. The remembering self takes precedence over the experiencing self. Yet, we are that past; it possesses us.

Time is a contradiction that leaves us perplexed and fearful. Oedipus was punished for delving too deeply into his past, much like Lot's wife in the story of Genesis. As Lot and his wife fled the burning city of Sodom, God instructed them not to look back. However, Lot's wife disobeyed and was transformed into a pillar of salt. To further explore the intricacies of time and memory, we can examine the captivating dialogue between Lot and God, as imagined by Polish philosopher Leszek Kolakowski.

Chagrined by the loss of his wife, Lot questions God's prohibition against looking back. God explains that one's entire past defines one's existence, and witnessing its destruction would be equivalent to ceasing to exist. Lot is puzzled: if looking at one's past and not looking at one's past both lead to nonexistence, does it imply certain death either way? God replies that self-contradiction is part of divine mystery. Lot must learn to carry his past while simultaneously pretending it is absent. Although this seems impossible, not a few have managed it. 'Long live not a few!' Kolakowski concludes.[27]

We all inhabit time's contra-diction and accept it as normal. The present is all that exists, yet we delve into our past as if it held greater importance. Language provides clues for understanding this relationship. The word 'present' conceals the most significant aspect of the connection between being and time. The Latin term *pra-essentia* translates to 'preceding essence' or 'facing essence'. This Latin word is a readaptation of the Greek *par-ousia*, also meaning 'facing being'. The Greek term eventually entered the Bible as 'Parousia', signifying the Second Coming of the Lord, or the presence of God in the present time.

The *essentia* in *pra-essentia* elevates the present time above the past and the future. In other words, the past is not situated in the past; it is the past. The future does not reside in the future; it is the future. Both the past and the future are encompassed within the essence of the present, which offers us the complete essence of time.[28]

The present serves as the primary horizon where being unfolds at every moment. As we will explore further, being is essentially time and nothing else. With music as an example, we see that time brings order to it; music exists insofar as it is united in a harmonious symphony of time. However, this is not the time of nature or the external universe; rather, it is our own inner time.

We are time itself. Through our very existence, we establish order in the world around us in time. We bestow upon this world the musical tempo it lacks but desperately needs. This tempo of life is deeply ingrained in a single verb: 'to be'.

Time Is a Verb

In principio erat Verbum. (In the beginning was the *verb*)

(John 1:1)

Time is order and nothing but order. And all order is time.

—Bachelard

The well-known expression, 'time is of the essence', holds within it a profound meaning regarding the inseparable relationship between time and being. However, time should not be interpreted in the conventional sense, such as 'clock time', but rather from a more fundamental perspective: that of being itself. We can also refer to this as order.

Time, being, and order weave themselves into the very fabric of our existence, becoming one and the same in both physics and philosophy. This intricate connection is not only reflected in language but also serves as the underlying foundation for our stories and our understanding of the world.

In the beginning, there is time. Our stories unfold, with phrases like 'once upon a time', 'since the beginning of time', or 'since time immemorial' setting the stage. Space becomes secondary, as time takes precedence in establishing order and coherence in our narratives. The biblical expression 'in the beginning was the word' emphasizes the temporal nature of language, free from spatial constraints. We may easily overlook space, but time remains essential in our storytelling.

Language thrives in the realm of time. Kierkegaard astutely observes that 'language has time as its element; all other media have space as their element'.[29] Rooted in the magical and orderly word 'to be', language is ordered in time. Consequently, the question 'where?' becomes less crucial than the fundamental question 'when?'

Being, encapsulated in the word 'is', is a metaphor we can grasp by positioning it in time. This persistent notion of being stands against time, or rather, within it. The motif of 'standing' resonates through the rich panorama of European languages, all tracing their lineage to Latin roots.[30] Time is what ex-sists: 'stands forth'. We call that phenomenon: *a situation*.

We often ask, 'In what *state* of mind are you?' instead of 'how are you?' or 'What is her *status* in the organization?' rather than 'Who is she in the organization?' Being 'takes a stand' to exist, in every situation. To understand being, one must stand under it, yet while we stare at being all the time, we perceive neither being nor time — only their hidden interplay. Being is preoccupied with standing and existing in contrast to the chaos of non-being. Standing can only be understood when juxtaposed with its opposite: time. This opposition gives rise to expressions like 'making time stand still'.

Ultimately, being symbolizes the passage of time. Declaring something 'is' acknowledges its impermanence. As day contrasts with night, being is distinguished by its opposition to non-being. Time isn't a linear sequence, but a moment that prompts being to stand and 'take place'.

Existentialism, the twentieth-century philosophical school popularized by Sartre, contends that to be human is to be in time; or more precisely, to be time itself. Roquentin, Sartre's introspective observer, articulates the unsettling relationship between being and time: 'this is time, time laid bare, coming slowly into existence, keeping us waiting, and when it does come, it makes us sick because we realize it's been already there for a long time.' His reflections on time and the world around him induce nausea, as he comprehends that his notions of past, present, and future are nonlinear, with time forever playing its peculiar game. Time can never be seized or understood, yet it remains omnipresent and defines everything. This idea is further reinforced by the linguistic duality in Sartre's native French, where 'I am' (*je suis*) can also mean 'I follow' (*je suis*), highlighting the intimate link between being and time.

In Mann's *The Magic Mountain*, Hans Castorp's contemplations on time illustrate the notion that our perception of time is dictated not by clocks but by the language we employ to describe it. Castorp experiments with linguistic definitions of time to understand its inner passage, recognizing that external clocks are often disconnected from our true experience of time.[31] The Berghof patients in the Swiss Alps exemplify this phenomenon, living on a grander scale of months rather than the minute notions of hours, days, or weeks. The magical quality of the Berghof is in its detachment from clock and calendar time, allowing patients to experience being as it unfolds 'naturally', without the constraints imposed by the ever-ticking clock. This detachment from conventional timekeeping grants a sense of freedom, unattainable in the ordinary clock-bound life, and relies on the way one speaks about time.

Nietzsche's poetic reverberations in 'Against Laws' dismantle the clock-bound constraints of time:

From now on, around my neck,
A little clock hangs by a thread:
The sun and stars stop in their tracks,
No cock crows, shadows are not cast,
And what was once declared by time,
To me us now deaf, dumb, and blind —

Despite our steady old tick-tock,
Nature knows no law or clock.[32]

The key phrase, 'what was once declared by time', at first shedding light on time's enigma, has turned 'deaf, dumb, and blind': hidden and forgotten. Shortly, we will retrace our steps to the word that captured and declared the original meaning of 'time'.

But essentially, the clock marches on forever in a circle, it is our own time, however, which is running out. The realization that the mystery of time is hidden in the word 'being' sheds new light on our understanding of existence. By examining the grammatical nature of 'to be', we uncover the crucial role that time plays in our language and perception. As a verb, 'to be' always operates within a tense, reflecting the temporal nature of our experience. This linguistic phenomenon is evident in the German term for verb, *das Zeitwort*, which literally means 'time-word'.

This close relationship between being and time in language suggests that our understanding of existence is intrinsically linked to our experience and perception of time. When we use the word 'to be', we are, in effect, organizing our existence and memory within the framework of time. As Carlo Rovelli's *The Order of Time* asserts, time is not an external phenomenon to be studied but rather an inherent part of our being. More like a philosopher than a quantum physicist, Rovelli writes that time is 'that which is capable of giving rise to what we are: beings made of time. That to which we owe our being, giving us the precious gift of our very existence'.[33]

By examining the linguistic and grammatical aspects of 'to be', we gain insight into the fundamental connection between being and time. We realize that the essence of our existence is not separate from time but deeply intertwined with it. Time is the organizing principle of our experience, memory, and ultimately, our being. Our understanding of ourselves, our world, and our place within it is profoundly shaped by the language we use to describe and make sense of time.

Time, then, is the underlying fabric of language, interwoven with our every utterance and thought. It becomes impossible to separate language from verbs, as verbs inherently embody time. We are reminded that 'verb', from the Latin *verbum*, originally meant 'word'. When we speak or think, we engage with time, a notion that pervades our language and shapes our experiences.

Indeed, if language were to convey a single message, it would be a call to action: 'Time is running out: Live! Be! Time to exist!' Language, with the time-word 'to be' at its heart, encapsulates our fundamental concern for time. Steiner's assertion that 'the status of the future of the verb is at the core of existence'[34] captures the essence of our preoccupation with time. As he suggests, the inflection of verbs becomes our 'skin and natural topography',[35] reflecting the ever-changing, yet contra-dictory nature of time.

This temporal aspect of language is highlighted by the distinction between imperfective and perfective verbs.[36] Imperfective verbs, such as 'to breathe' or 'to live', describe continuous actions with no clear end, while perfective verbs represent activities with definite endpoints, like reading, walking, talking, and playing. Languages employ complex verb systems, including perfect tenses, to help us navigate time and plan for the future.

Intriguingly, some languages, like the Piraha language of the Amazon, defy the conventional understanding of perfective verbs and time. The Piraha people, living in a linguistic world devoid of perfect tenses, experience time differently, focusing solely on the present moment. This 'immediacy of experience', as linguist Daniel Everett, who studied the Piraha language described it, shapes their entire worldview, affecting their perceptions of history and even the divine.[37]

Aristotle and other philosophers have long recognized the crucial role verbs play in expressing time and animating ideas. According to Humboldt, it is only through the verb that an idea 'steps forth into the realm of reality'. Foucault, too, emphasized the connection between grammar and our understanding of time and space.[38] Our sense of location, we will come to argue, is fundamentally grounded in time, rather than space.

In examining the verb 'to be', we uncover a profound connection to time, often overlooked due to its continuous and imperfective nature. Like 'to walk' and 'walking', the verb 'to be' transforms into 'being', revealing the temporality and finitude of existence. As we walk, we continue until we stop; as we exist, we continue until we cease to be.

This inherent limitation of time is the bedrock of our understanding of human existence. As Augustine observed, 'Not everything grows old, but everything dies.'[39] To be human is to recognize the temporality of our existence and embrace the beauty found within the scarcity of time. Our language reflects this understanding, weaving time into every thought and utterance.

Mortals Are Immortal

I seem to have such strength in me now, that I think I could stand anything, any suffering, only to be able to say and to repeat to myself every moment, 'I exist' [...] Whether I see the sun or not, I know that it is there. And to know that the sun is there — is not this a whole life in itself?

—Dostoevsky

Existentialism, at first glance, might present itself as a rather sombre philosophy, emphasizing mortality and the limited duration of our existence. However, let us examine the other side of this coin, revealing the vibrant aspect of being: life itself.

If our existence were not tethered to time, it would dissolve into the vast expanse. The fundament of being is its intricate engagement with time. An unbounded, eternal being would hurl us back to a primordial state of chaos, void, and nothingness. The most expansive and vacuous concept is the timeless nothing: the void, but not being. Language bestows upon being the gift of the word, signifying a specific, time-bound entity. Eternity may be vast and empty, but what truly interests us is being, anchored in the temporal realm.

The notion of nothing depends on its counterpart: being. The fabric of nature requires opposing forces: chaos and order, life and death, day and night, light and darkness, matter and antimatter, speech and silence, being and nothing.

Heraclitus, the pre-Socratic philosopher, discerned the duality of nature, composed of opposites. His *Fragments* feature complex and seemingly contradictory aphorisms: 'From the strain of binding opposites comes harmony'; 'Two made one are never one. Arguing the same we disagree. Singing together we compete. We choose each other to be one, and from the one both soon diverge'; 'Without injustices, the name of justice would mean what?'[40]

For those preoccupied with the enigma of being, Heraclitus presents an intriguing statement: 'the immortals are mortal, the mortals immortal, each living in the other's death and dying in the other's life.' Mortals, it seems, are immortal, not because they defy death, but because they embody being. They possess being precisely because they confront death. Their very existence unfolds within the temporary horizon, stretched between the eternal, meaningless nothing and its lively negation as being.

Death, the antithesis of life, renders existence feasible. Every fleeting moment negates its own passing. Bachelard posits, 'Although time will no doubt be reborn, it must first die.'[41] Justice devoid of injustice is hollow, and life, unaccompanied by death, carries no weight. The eternal question lingers: ought we to live our death as immortals or die our life as mortals? Life demands mortality. Simultaneity remains unattainable. Devoid of the boundaries erected by time, life and human existence would lack purpose. The questions arise: why rise now and not later? Why select this over that? Why navigate a life-path if existence stretches into an unending road without an ultimate terminus? Being is a scarce resource, and therein lies its intrinsic worth.

Time's inexorable passage infuses meaning and authenticity into our existence. In its original Greek context, *afthentis* bore a morbid overtone, denoting 'committing suicide' or 'murdering with one's own hands'. For the Greeks, authenticity required taking a stand, making an irrevocable choice, embracing one path whilst relinquishing others. Authenticity and meaning necessitate definitiveness, limitation, and non-negotiability, attainable solely through the temporal dimensions that bind our existence.

Kierkegaard contends that the most profound moments of pleasure are intimately intertwined with death. He writes, 'This is the main defect with everything human, that it is only through opposition that the object of desire is possessed.'[42] The paramount object of desire, the concern for our existence, emerges through its antithesis: non-being or death. Yet, a preoccupation with death also embodies a preoccupation with life.

The constraints imposed by the temporal dimension forge life into a tangible entity: our existence. This limitation ensures that each choice bears significance. Time infuses meaning, even into the options we ultimately reject, urging us to discern the most favourable alternatives. It functions as a price tag for our actions and choices, assigning opportunity costs to all facets of life, a vital aspect of what we perceive as 'meaning'.

Music, that quintessentially human expression of meaning, derives its order and intelligibility from the temporal dimension. Yet, music is not the sole meaningful 'product' shaped by time's passage. Light, an even more vital manifestation of existence, acquires depth and meaning when we interpret it through our temporal perception. Phenomenological and existentialist perspectives emphasize the human experience, positing that light occupies a unique place in our lives, revealing meaning and illuminating existence. Like music, light demands structure, and akin to existence, it unfolds with or against time.

Light inhabits the instant of time: the *situation*. The Latin *in-stare* signifies 'to stand in', intriguingly portraying the temporal dimension via a spatial metaphor. Conventionally, time moves, while space 'stands', perceivable in a specific position. Objects: a lamp, a tree, a building, stand in space. But what permits us to perceive the lamp, the tree, and the comprehensive 'world picture' as situated in space? What enables the totality of existence to be under-stood?

Elegantly simple: light. In its absence, nothing can be seen or exist. Analogous to music, light is a pure expression of time and order, influenced by human existence. Time not only orchestrates music's symphony but also situates light within space. The unrivalled swiftness of light creates the illusion of stillness. An illuminated chair appears static, yet it is the light that moves, drawing attention. The light's movement goes unnoticed because, in essence, one embodies that movement; one is time itself, existing within space. What is essentially *going on*? The essence itself: light *goes on* space.

The journey from the dynamic Greek concept of *morphe* to its Latin successor 'form' provides an exciting perspective on how language impacts our perception of the world. This transition signifies a shift from valuing change to appreciating stability, carrying significant implications for understanding reality.

Consider this passage in Plato's *Republic*:

And the soul is like the eye: when resting upon that on which truth and being shine, the soul perceives and understands and is radiant with intelligence; but when turned towards the twilight of becoming and perishing, then she has opinion only, and goes blinking about, and is first of one opinion and then of another, and seems to have no intelligence?[43]

What Plato is contrasting through Socrates' words here is 'intelligence' *resting* on being versus mere 'opinion' *blinking about* on becoming. In other words, we don't say we under-*move* becoming, but rather we under-*stand* being. Perceiving light as form renders it stationary, yet its true essence lies in movement: the instantaneous speed of light. Heraclitus' aphorism, 'the only constant is change', holds true. Light transcends space; it is time. Space, immersed in light, radiates or 'shines' toward us. Time enables the comprehension of space, and without it, space would vanish. We shall come back to this interplay between space and time later on.

As a metaphor for being, light is a potent symbol spanning cultures. Through this transformed form, we grasp the essence of being in its most fundamental yet delicate manifestations.

Let There Be Light!

*Where other animals walk on all fours and look
to the ground,
man was given a towering head and commanded
to stand erect,
with his face uplifted to gaze on the stars of heaven.*

—Ovid

In the annals of human history, mythology and religion, light has consistently occupied a central and enigmatic position. Thinkers and poets, such as Heraclitus and Ovid, conceived fire, the primordial emblem of light, as the world's origin. In Greek mythology, Prometheus, whose name implies 'forethinking' or 'original thinking', stole fire from the gods, enduring punishment for his transgression. The association of fire, flame and light with the most elemental aspects of human experience is unmistakable.

The Greek term for 'human', *Anthropos*, means 'the one looking upwards', reflecting the quintessential nature of humans as always gazing toward the sky's brightest star. This star symbolizes the primary source of light, which unifies humanity.

A deep reverence for light pervades various cultures and religious traditions, often manifested in sun worship. The sun's warmth and light have bound (*religare*) humanity since time immemorial. In Ancient Egypt, for example, the sun god Ra was deemed the progenitor of all creation. Egyptians venerated the scarab, a sacred creature, for its connection to the sun's divine emergence at dawn.

Zoroastrianism narrates the creation of the universe by the supreme god Ahura Mazda, assisted by the twin spirits Spenta Mainyu and Angra Mainyu. These spirits symbolize the dichotomy of light and darkness, truth and deceit, life and death. In some Iranian dialects, Ahura Mazda's name is synonymous with the sun, emphasizing light's crucial role in religious customs.[44]

Hinduism and Ancient Greek culture furnish further instances of sun worship. The Hindu swastika signifies the sun's movement, while Ancient Greeks revered Apollo, the god of the sun and light. Apollo's name denotes the sun-god who dispels chaos and nothingness with his creative light, ushering in order and life.[45]

Christianity subtly incorporates sun worship, as God the Father becomes the 'light of the world'. Some contend that Jesus' birthdate, December 25, was adopted from Mithraism, a competing religion in the Roman Empire's waning days.[46] Presently, Sunday remains Christianity's most significant day, commemorating Christ's resurrection as 'the light of the world'.[47]

Judaism and Islam, the other two Abrahamic faiths, also centre their primary rituals around the sun. The Judaic Shabbat, signifying 'rest' or 'ceasing from work', commences every Friday at sunset, while in Islam, one of the five mandatory prayers (the Fajr prayer) starts at sunrise. Across diverse cultures and religions, light's pivotal role unites humanity, providing a common thread weaving through our shared experiences and convictions.

Humans have long been attracted to the sun, and its bright radiance on a cloudless sky uplifts our spirits. All our gods may be considered poetic metaphors for the sun in the sky, and for good reason. The sun is the Supreme Being, the ultimate God; it bestows light and life upon us, it is what it is, it exists independently (Yahweh). As the source of light for all earth's living creatures, especially for us, the ones looking upwards, the sun holds a unique position.

Our relationship with light is distinct and unparalleled compared to animals, which often see in low light or complete darkness. Yet we require as much light as possible. Unlike *Athene noctua*, the European owl symbolizing wisdom due to its ability to see in the dark, we perceive nothing in pitch darkness. For us, everything that exists necessitates illumination for comprehension. It demands light, clarity. Thus, we understand being by standing under the sun.

However, the sun offers more than being; it also provides time: specifically, the present time. Illuminating all things and objects shining in the world, the sun, akin to a projector in a film, *presents* the entire world to our view in the present moment. If life were a movie titled 'Being', then the sun would be the principal projector, presenting it to us through its light.

Heraclitus' earlier statement, 'nature loves to hide', can be equally applied to the sun's role and the light it delivers. The sun is a concealed God because we cannot gaze at it directly without being blinded. The sun can observe us, but we can never return its gaze. Concerning its light, it remains hidden in plain sight, as we do not see the light itself; we only see the objects and things it illuminates. The paradox lies in the fact that light is nothing in itself, yet it offers us everything through itself. It necessitates things to shine upon. The *morphe* of light conceals itself behind every *form* it bestows upon things.

In his tome *A Brief History of the Verb To Be*, Italian linguist Andrea Moro uncovers an elusive connection between light and being: 'A nothing, illuminated by another nothing, becomes something.'[48] Like the unseen verb 'to be' that bestows existence to all else, light remains unseen, revealing only its effects on the world. In absence of being or light, only chaos reigns: the void, the darkness.

Scientific parlance dubs a 'something' seen in the light as a 'substance'. The Latin *sub-stare* hints at 'standing-under'. Under what? The light and the sun, of course. Similarly, the Chinese word for 'thing' (*dongxi*) translates to 'East-West', implying the location under the sun, following the light's swirl from East to West. Colloquially speaking, when something is *going on*, it's the 'is' that's moving: the light illuminating the world below.

Being and time tango together, crafting the order of the world around us. *Sub-stare* indicates the interplay under the light, while *in-stare* captures the instant of time (light) that situates it in space, shining with being towards us. The sun takes centre stage, bestowing existence and clarity upon our world, reminding us that we do, indeed, exist.

When Yahweh declared, 'Let there be light!', He might as well have proclaimed, 'Let there be being!' or simply, 'Let there be...' For light exists only when it shines upon something. Thus, being and light are inseparable partners. The light reflects itself upon something (or someone), and that someone is us — the human beings, the interpreters of all things shining in the light.

It is the human, that 'holier living creature, more able to think high thoughts', as Ovid quipped, who unravels the mysteries of being. While standing under the sun's divine light, our lofty thoughts reach towards it. Is the *highest* thought then, one of being?

Shakespeare grapples with the intricacies of human existence:

For beauty, wit,
High birth, vigour of bone, desert in service,
Love, friendship, charity, are subjects all
To envious and calumniating Time.
One touch of nature makes the whole world kin,
That all with one consent praise new-born gawds,
Though they are made and moulded of things past,
And give to dust that is a little gilt
More laud than gilt o'er-dusted.
The present eye praises the present object.
Then marvel not, thou great and complete man,
That all the Greeks begin to worship Ajax;
Since things in motion sooner catch the eye
Than what not stirs.[49]

Shakespeare masterfully conveys profound messages in just a few lines, revealing the nature of time as envious and calumniating. Time seems envious of its own expiry, desiring to persist and withstand change. Our language captures this sentiment, reflecting a deep and primordial longing to hold onto time and being. As long as we exist, we counter nothingness with being, triumphing over death, chaos, and disorder. We exclaim to the empty and chaotic nature that It is! Order is! Being is!

The Bard further alludes to the sun in the sky, describing it as the 'one touch of nature' that unites the world. This touch of light moulds and shapes the new-born gods from the past. In various languages, the interconnected nature of the world and light is evident. For instance, in Slavic languages, the roots of 'world' and 'light' share similarities. Phrases like 'to be in the world' in Polish, Russian or Czech, translate directly as 'to be in the light', (*svet, swiat*) illustrating the significance of light in our understanding of the world.

Language continues to be our guide in this exploration of being and time, with words like *maintenant* ('now' in French) and *Stunde* ('hour' in German) revealing our preoccupation with grasping the fleeting nature of time.[50] While the word 'instant' further emphasizes the paradoxical nature of time, as it 'stands by disappearing',[51] a concept echoed by Heidegger's observation that 'time persists, consists in passing. It is, in that it constantly is not'.[52]

Rovelli's poetic insight that the world is sketched in dots by a 'light hand' highlights the intricate relationship between light and our perception of reality.[53] Pointillist artists, like Seurat and Van Gogh, captured the essence of light in space long before philosophers and scientists unravelled its mysteries. Their masterpieces, composed of countless light dots, portrayed reality as an instantaneous event: a snapshot of time, brilliantly illuminated.

Indeed, art has a unique ability to foresee scientific breakthroughs, as McLuhan posits that pointillists were painting the concept of television long before its invention.[54] The similarities between their artwork and modern TV screens or computer monitors are striking, as both rely on numerous tiny light sources to create images.[55] This transformation of moving time into static frames mirrors the way we perceive reality, with each instant building upon the next to shape our perception of the world.[56]

Shakespeare, once again, grasped the intricate connection between space and time. Hamlet's encounter with his father's ghost from the past reveals a profound understanding of the unity of space and time:

The time is out of joint.
O cursed spite,
That ever I was born to set it right!

His desire 'to set it right' implies an attempt to pause time, capturing the past in the present moment. Space, as a manifestation of lost time, functions as a vessel for memory. We experience space through the lens of elapsed time, recognizing that our world is a product of countless instants woven together by the thread of memory.

As Bachelard states in his *Poetics of Space*, 'At times we think we know ourselves in time, when all we know is a sequence of fixations in the spaces of the being's stability — a being who does not want to melt away, and who, even in the past, when he sets out in search of things past, wants time to "suspend" its flight. In its countless alveoli space contains compressed time. That is what space is for.'[57]

Space as Metamorphosed Time

They evidently do not know that you are everywhere. No space circumscribes you. You alone are always present even to those who have taken themselves far from you.

—Augustine

'By dying one becomes the despot of the world',[58] wrote Cioran, playfully exploring the word 'despot' in its clever English translation. In death, one de-spots the spot, transcends the confines of space; time brings an end to it. Without time, space loses its meaning.

We tend to think of space as a static, unchanging entity. It seems to remain constant regardless of our presence. Yet, space is not merely form, but *morphe*. Like time, space is something we inhabit and experience. The phrase 'once upon a time' acknowledges the connection between time and space, as human presence defines both. And just as something can 'take time', it can also 'take place'. Being is going on in space as long as there is presence: the present of time.

Consider the words we use to describe space: here and there. Upon closer examination, these terms are vague and indeterminate. The distinction between them is blurred, highlighting the fluidity of our concept of space. Bachelard refers to here and there as 'unfortunate adverbs' with 'unsupervised powers', emphasizing their interchangeable usage.[59]

What do we mean when we say 'here'? Does it refer to the ground beneath our feet, a few metres away, within this city, or on this planet? Any of these definitions could be valid. Similarly, what does 'there' mean? Is it slightly further away, 10 metres distant, in another city, or on another planet? Once again, any of these interpretations could apply. We find ourselves perplexed: how can 'here' and 'there' be indistinguishable? How can the entire space we call our 'world' be both here and there simultaneously? Indeed, the world is here, there, and everywhere. When we claim to be in the world, are we everywhere at once? In a sense, we are and we aren't. Language, the tool we use to express and understand our world, fails to adequately define the spatial relationships that surround us. The once firm boundaries between here and there dissolve, leaving us adrift in a sea of ambiguity.

Thomas Mann asks: 'There? Where is there? How far, how near? You cannot tell. Dizzyingly it escapes your measurement … Your eye grows dim with uncertainty, for in yourself you have no sense-organ to help you judge of time or space.'[60]

The subjectivity of near and far, here and there, challenges the significance we attribute to these distinctions. Our perception of space is like a metaphor; the essence remains the same while the form changes. Something big and far is metaphorically transferred in our sight as small but near. Optical illusions, such as the Ames room illusion, demonstrate this phenomenon. Even distant objects can be perceived as 'here', further blurring the lines between here and there. This confusion dissolves when we shift our focus from space to time as the primary measure of being.

So, what anchors us in this vast expanse? It is not space, but rather time that serves as the guiding principle of our experience. No matter how far away something might be, it exists in the present, the eternal instant that unites all living beings. Our perceptions of space are mutable and fluid, while the present moment remains constant, a steady heartbeat in the midst of chaos.

In the digital realm, this concept becomes even more evident. As we traverse the virtual landscapes of 'cyber-space', we are not navigating physical distances, but rather temporal connections. When we communicate with someone on the opposite side of the planet, we speak to their present, *instantaneous* self. Time, and its instant, unifies us in the same presence. Distance becomes irrelevant when the instant of time places us within the same essence of the present. On-line interactions occur in time, not exactly on-earth; hence, the term 'cyber-space' should be more accurately referred to as 'cyber-time'.

Our brains are wired to perceive the world through spatial constructs, but time remains an elusive entity that we struggle to comprehend. This difficulty is compounded by the fact that we use spatial language to describe temporal concepts, further obscuring the distinction between the two.

For instance, the instant, or *in-stare*, represents the time that sets space in place here and now, in the present. Distance, or *di-stare*, signifies the duplication of the instant, transposing the here into there. By merging two distances into a single instant, space and distance vanish, transforming there into everywhere. Time and space are inextricably linked, as space represents the stage on which the drama of time unfolds.

In the *interesting* play between being and being (essence and essence), time weaves its subtle, hidden magic. It unites us in the shared experience of the ever-present instant, connecting us across the expanse of distance and conjuring the mirage of space.

Being stretches only *as far as we are concerned*. The span of being extends from the 'first' person on the planet to the 'last', whoever or wherever we imagine them to be. Rovelli muses: 'we can easily consider our entire planet to be like a single bubble where we can speak of the present as if it were an instant shared by us all. This is as far as we can go.'[61] If, by some cosmic whim, all human beings vanished from the planet, so too would time, the instant, and hence, all distance evaporate. And without these, without space and time, wouldn't we be left, indeed, with no-thing?

For where there are no present people, there can be no present things, and thus, there is, strictly speaking, nothing beyond human presence. And where there is no is, nothing is afoot. So, let the nothing proceed gracefully without us! Why? Because we are not interested in nothing. What we are interested in is: essence, being.

In our attempts to grasp the enigmatic nature of time, we resort to spatial metaphors, inadvertently conflating the two. Our language struggles to describe time, as we tend to think of it in spatial terms. Lakoff points out that using spatial words like 'in' and 'at' for time expressions (e.g., in an hour, at ten o'clock) makes sense because we tend to think of time in terms of space.[62] This confusion may come from the fact that our minds think in images that are more easily visualized in spatial terms than temporal ones.

'Geometry', Buonomano explains. 'was one of the first true scientific fields for a reason: science is much simpler if one can get away with ignoring time. [...] The mathematics available to the Greek philosophers and scientists was not well suited to studying how things change over time.'[63] Science has difficulty grasping something that is both something and nothing: time is hiding behind space, *all-ways*.

Augustine's perplexing question, 'What, then, is time? If no one asks me, I know what it is. If I wish to explain it to him who asks me, I do not know',[64] underscores the difficulties inherent in describing time. As we attempt to define time, our language relies on spatial metaphors, further entangling time and space.

We employ a myriad of metaphors to articulate time, projecting it onto motion, stillness, or placement in space (time passes, time stands still, time goes forward, chasing time, time is money, Father Time). And yet, like Augustine, we remain challenged to describe time without invoking space. Language is still in its infancy when it comes to time, it is speechless about it. And perhaps, it will always remain so.

Recognizing the impossibility of accurately defining time through language, Augustine suggests that the conventional division of time into past, present, and future is flawed. Instead, he posits that only the present truly exists.[65] As we accept this common usage, we come to realize that time is the essence of being, the quintessential presence at the heart of all existence. 'Man's concept is spirit', says Kierkegaard, 'and we must not allow ourselves to be put off by the fact that he is also able to walk on two legs.'

A Luminous Situation

The waking have one world in common. Sleepers meanwhile turn aside, each into a darkness of his own.

—Heraclitus

Our very existence is entwined with the sun's radiance and the flow of time. As the Bard says, 'One touch of nature makes the whole world kin', signifying that our connections lie not in geographic locations, but in the luminous present moment shared by all.

The sun, akin to a musician or a disco ball, unites us through a common experience of time. This bond is forged not through sound, but through light — through presence, as beings coexist. Gathering-around-being means being-to-gether: we inhabit the same temporal space, like attendees at a grand celebration of existence. As long as the music of being plays, the party of existence lasts as long as we are present in it or at it, whichever preposition fits best.

Time situates us in the present, an instant shared with all others. Shakespeare termed this shared experience the 'one consent', a mutual recognition of each other's presence under the light. Nothing unites us more profoundly and unconditionally than light, which binds us in a religious manner simply by sharing the same illumination. Could time be the most religious, unseen force in existence? And how do we commonly comprehend the term 'time'?

The word 'time' derives from the Indo-European word *di* or *dai*, meaning 'to divide'. A clock epitomizes this concept, slicing time into hours, minutes, and seconds to facilitate organization and partitioning of our daily lives. Before mechanical division, the primary segmentation of time was natural; the distinction between day and night, with the sun as the original clock. As Heraclitus observed, 'The sun is the timekeeper of the day and seasons which oversees all things.'[66]

The word 'day'[67] likely evolved from this ancient term, which denoted 'time' and the only time. The *dai* represents the entire universe — one solar rotation until darkness descends. While day represented time, night did not; it marked time's cessation and the world's *end*. The world ended not with a final Judgement Day or Apocalypse, but each time the sun vanished below the horizon: *for the time being*.[68] Various languages even incorporate negation into the word 'night' (night/naught; nacht/

nicht; nuit/néant).[69] Night's *nothingness* unleashes humanity's dual nature, as we indulge in love, intoxication, dance, sin, and crime, feeling liberated and concealed from the sun's omnipresent gaze. Thus, night reveals our multifaceted selves, for better or worse. Kierkegaard: 'I toast you, dark night, I toast you as victor, and this is my solace, for you make everything shorter, the day, time, life, and memory's tribulation, in eternal oblivion!'

The night undoes the shared world that connects us through light and time. It rejects the 'time' of day, real time, and denies the universe its existence. Ancient Greeks grasped this well. In their mythology, the goddess of the night, Nyx, was the daughter of chaos and the mother of ether and day. They recognized that day emerged from night, being arose from nothingness, and order and goodness sprouted from chaos and malevolence.

Initially, the night was deemed 'not time' due to the darkness that rendered activity nearly impossible. In those early days, with scarce illumination, one could barely perceive anything, there was no world to observe, share, or engage with. Venturing anywhere or undertaking any action at night was treacherous, if not unattainable. Only in the seventeenth century did streetlights emerge in major European cities like Paris, the first 'city of lights', encouraging nocturnal activity. Until then, however, the night was demonized. Jesus stated: 'Are there not twelve hours of daylight? If anyone walks around in the daytime, he does not stumble, because he sees the light of this world. But if anyone walks around at night, he stumbles, because the light is not in him' (John 11:10). The word 'journey', from the French *journée* (day, a day's travel), reiterates that travel was initially limited to daylight hours.

Christ subsequently claimed the light for himself: 'I am the light of the world. Whoever follows me will not walk in darkness, but will have the light of life' (John: 8:12). Daylight symbolizes life, divinity, and goodness, while the darkness of night connotes death and wickedness. The night is frequently associated with the origin of all 'dark, evil forces', the time when nightmares transpire. The night is a non-world or even an underworld. Consequently, God is not merely a voice but also the light that rescues us from the darkness and malevolence of the night. In the absence of our most prominent and brilliant *astra* in the sky, we are left with nothing but *dis-aster*.

The sun lies at the heart of our ability to orient ourselves in both space and time. It is why we call the East, where the sun rises, the 'Orient'. The Orient provides our primary orientation in geographical space, and the other three geographical coordinates, West, North, and South, also rely on the sun's position.[70] Essentially, our entire geographical and scientific localization in space depends on the sun. Without this star, we would be astray, unable to determine where or when we are: a truly disastrous situation.

The Australian Aboriginal tribe Kuuk Thaayorre possesses a unique language that lacks the concepts of 'left' and 'right'.[71] Instead, they precisely locate anything in the world in relation to the sun at any given moment. For them, a hand is not simply a 'left hand' or 'right hand' — its designation depends on how one turns toward the sun. What is always the 'left hand' for us can change to 'South-East' now and 'North-West' in the next moment for the Kuuk Thaayorre people. Their existence, in the truest sense of the word, is tethered to the sun, as their being as a location is directly determined by it.

In industrialized societies, we have delegated this task to technology. However, without the sun rising in the East at the exact same place and time every day, our geographical maps, sophisticated GPS systems, and even our most precise atomic clocks would instantly fail. It is logical, then, to revere the sun, as it is the most crucial and reliable source for our primary measurements of space and time. The sun holds the highest standard in our entire value system. If human existence prioritizes anything, the sun would undoubtedly be 'up there' on our list of values.

Bachelard reminds us that 'the sun is, primarily, the great Light of the World. [...] Upper light, being the principle of centrality, is a very important value in the hierarchy of images. For the imagination, therefore, the world gravitates about a value'.[72] This brings us back to metaphors. The sun, both literally and metaphorically, holds the highest value in the entire universe, and everything living beneath it, all subjects and substances, looks up to it.

Our language and numerous religious and non-religious rituals reflect this upward trajectory. The metaphors for 'up' often relate to something 'good', 'powerful', or 'desirable'.[73] We say: 'this is uplifting', 'I am upbeat', 'she enjoys a high status', 'wages are going up', 'he needs a raise', and so on. Everything good and holy reaches up toward the sun in the sky, as when we hold our hands up in prayer or at a concert. God, as the highest value of being, had to be up there, with the Devil, his nemesis, down in the underworld. It appears the sun, indeed, is the God of all metaphors.

The Great Noon: A Zarathustran Tale

There was a man sent from God, whose name was John. He was not the light, but a witness to the light.

(John 1:1, 6–9)

Enter Zarathustra, not sent by God, but the sun's chosen messenger, heralding the end of divinity and the dawn of the 'overman'. Nietzsche played with the biblical bond between hearing and obedience, crafting his Zarathustra, a prophet of a godless new beginning.

The title of Nietzsche's famous book *Thus Spoke Zarathustra* is not chosen at random: even though Nietzsche was writing it, his

Zarathustra was instead speaking for him through the written pages. Thus Spoke Zarathustra! Each chapter deliberately concludes with this echo, a playful nod to the recurring nature of biblical teachings. Nietzsche's Zarathustra, a man, not a deity, leads the charge towards a superman without God, a being illuminated by the sun alone, without a divine metaphor.

What better place for Zarathustra's tale to commence than a heart-to-heart with the sun in the sky? 'You great star! What would your happiness be if you had not those for whom you shine?' A light unto the world, yet it is Zarathustra who is its foremost beneficiary: 'For ten years you have come up here to my cave: you would have tired of your light and of this route without me, my eagle and my snake.' He blesses the sun, as if it were divine, for the light shared with his eagle and snake, symbols of the sun's highest and wisest manifestations.

'Thus Zarathustra had spoken to his heart when the sun stood at noon, then he gazed at the sky with a questioning look, for above him he heard the sharp cry of a bird. And behold! An eagle cut broad circles through the air, and upon it hung a snake, not as prey but as a friend, for the snake curled itself around the eagle's neck.'[74]

An eagle circles overhead, a snake curled around its neck, an eternal dance of the sun's infinite cyclicality: yin and yang. Nietzsche's metaphorical sun, the eternal return, is the sole constant in a world of flux. The sun transcends time, and so we assign it the highest value. The sun, our God, our creator of metaphors, for 'around God everything becomes — what? perhaps a "world"?' asks Nietzsche in *Beyond Good and Evil*.[75] Yet Zarathustra, a mortal, must descend like a solar deity to share this new dawn with the masses. Like God, and like time itself, he does so in a paradoxical and contradictory way:

I want to bestow and distribute until the wise among human beings have once again enjoyed their folly, and the poor once again their wealth. For this, I must descend into the depths, as you do evenings when you go behind the sea and bring light even to the underworld, you super-rich star!

Much like the Grand Inquisitor's ingenious ex-communication of Jesus, Zarathustra does not merely insist; he forcefully demands to be forgotten by his followers:

> You say you believe in Zarathustra? But what matters Zarathustra! You are my believers, but what matter all believers! You had not yet sought yourselves, then you found me. [...] Now I bid you lose me and find yourselves; and only when you have all denied me will I return to you.

The 'great noon' looms, that singular moment uniting the world in a shared experience, the sun of knowledge standing at its zenith. Perhaps inspired by Homer's Proteus, the sea-god consulted only at midday, Zarathustra's noon becomes a symbol of the eternal present[76]:

> Dead are all gods: now we want the overman to live. — Let this be our last will at the great noon!

The sun, as the everlasting God, is the ever-present Today: a timelessness encompassing all yesterdays and tomorrows, the *nunc stans*. As Augustine says:

> Because 'your years do not fail', your years are one Today ... 'But you are the same'; and all tomorrow and hereafter, and indeed all yesterday and further back, you will make a Today, you have made a Today.[77]

In this great noon, through the transformative power of the present moment, humanity may transcend its current state and embrace the overman. The sun, both time and being, unites us all in its eternal presence, a Parousia and Praessentia, the sire of time and all beings. As the Alpha and the Omega, the sun, our eternal God, measures all our beginnings and ends, giving birth to 'new-born gawds' from the same eternally recurring star, framed in ever-changing forms and metaphors.

Finding Ourselves ... Present

Not a moment when I am not incredulous at finding myself in just that moment.

—Cioran

Let us earnestly respond to Zarathustra's summons to 'find ourselves'. For it is not self-evident that we truly do.

We shall commence at the outset. What transformed us into the *Anthropos*, those gazing skyward at the sun? At most, it was our astonishment; at the least, our unwavering attention. Attention, *ad tenere*, conveys 'to hold on to' or 'to behold'. The human being was captivated by the shining light from above: by beholding, he was held back in awe by his own being in the light. His mere presence dumbfounded and staggered him: his mission immediately became submission. By observing the celestial spectacle, he was serving it; or as we say, *paying attention* to it. Paying attention? With what currency? At the cost of understanding his own metaphoric, and even mysterious position in the observed.

From the very beginning, the nature of being was concealed from humans, making us the most interesting creatures of all. When we say 'interesting', we, once more, intend it literally. Humans dwell inter-essences: between their own essence and the world's. But one of them is always veiled. Perpetually absorbed in the external realm, they frequently disregard their inner selves. Humans ex-sist: they encounter something beyond themselves, fathoming the world more deeply than their own selves.

But do we possess a self? What signifies having a self? Regardless of the response, owning a self intimates a certain remove from that self. The persona, the mask of being, worn by the self, yet not identical to the self lurking behind. The 'self' wrestles with its existence. At times, we claim, 'I found myself pondering it', oblivious to employing both 'I' and 'self' as separate beings. Logically, the concept of discovering oneself appears contradictory; but existentially, it coheres. Dostoevsky's Raskolnikov exhibits that within each persona lies a *raskol*: a cleavage, a fissure, a duality, a Jekyll and Hyde.

'I am distinct from all my sensations', pens Cioran. 'I fail to understand how. I even fail to understand whose they are. Moreover, who is this I initiating the three propositions?'[78] Isn't it fascinating that we humans can recognize ourselves in the mirror? However, do we truly discover our selves *in* the physical mirror? The literal interpretation of this phrase is absurd, but our lives are not governed by literal, scientific, or physical principles; rather, they are guided by metaphor and poetry. The mirror serves as another metaphorical container projected in space. While we are not physically in the mirror, we confidently claim to be *in* it. Yet, who truly resides in the mirror? Is it the body (the 'I') that looks, or the image it discovers (the self)? Can one exist without the other? These existential questions pose a perplexing conundrum.

Now imagine the whole 'world' of space and time as a mirror: when unattended, the mirror ceases to reflect. The mirror's primary function of reflection is lost without our confrontation; nothing exists; nothing 'stands forth'. In this context, aren't terms like 'space' and 'time' themselves containers? Isn't the world itself a container in which we find ourselves? To which we pay attention?

But let us, for a moment, not pay attention. Keep the change of attention in our pockets, and we realize that we are not in a container, but rather in a rendezvous. A gathering we attend, featuring two parties: the I and the self. We are both the host and the most anticipated attendee. Existential presence is a one-person event. It is as if we usher our persona into this world by unveiling our presence within it, *in* that singular moment in time.

Thus, presence, the world of space and time, does not dwell in a vacuum. It is discovered. By us. The ones exploring for ourselves within it. Like King Oedipus unearthing his past to comprehend his present circumstance, human existence is a process of seeking and finding one's presence (participation) in being.

Gratefully, what we discern in our presence surpasses Oedipus' discovery (to our relief). What we unearth is nothing more and nothing less than a miracle. The most captivating question of all arises: Why does this convocation 'take place' at all? Why are we not simply absent? This inquiry stretches the limits of human rationality and argumentation, venturing into the domain of wonder and even astonishment.

Echoing the passage in Isaiah (29):

Be stunned and amazed,
blind yourselves and be sightless;
be drunk, but not from wine,
stagger, but not from beer.

No libation could make us reel from the sheer realization of our enigmatic presence in this world. When humanity first cried 'I am' into the vast, void cosmos and the light above, they genuinely found themselves for the first time. They confronted the miracle of their existence and presence in the world, a world in which they now sought a place. It was then they acknowledged their miraculous and unexplained presence as being. This mysterious existence in the world was the ultimate marvel, the question of all questions: 'Why am I present and not absent?' 'Why am I attending this event called being, and what ought I to do now that I find myself in it?' Human existence would be far less interesting without this profound and enigmatic query at its heart.

In Rilke's short poem 'The Night', he lauds the miraculous endowment of our existence and presence in this world. Intriguingly, Rilke devotes the poem not to daylight's brilliance but its antithesis: the obscurity of night. Only by recollecting the existence of absence (the poetic 'naught') can we treasure the wonder of presence: the light of day.

> You, darkness, of whom I am born—
> I love you more than the flame
> that limits the world
> to the circle it illuminates
> and excludes all the rest.

But the dark embraces everything:

> shapes and shadows, creatures and me,
> people, nations—just as they are.
> It lets me imagine
> a great presence stirring beside me.
> I believe in the night.

Rilke communicates that to grasp the essence of pure presence, we must believe in the night: the absence encircling it. To fathom being, we must also discern chaos and the void. A candle ignited in daylight lacks the potency of one lit in a dark chamber. By juxtaposing the darkness around the candle, we better appreciate its fragile yet forceful and significant flame of being and presence. Rilke beckons us to marvel at the fact of being itself, urging us to ponder the night, the darkness, to better comprehend the great presence *stirring* the whirlwind of the universe.

Zarathustra, Nietzsche's sage, astutely informed the sun it would tire of shining without him. Likewise, the world itself would tire of 'existing' without us. More so, akin to a vacant 'switched off' mirror when we are not facing it, the world bereft of us would lose its primary purpose: to have someone unearth their presence within it. Hence, the world may rightfully thank humanity, the sole creatures who seek and eventually find themselves in it, for bestowing meaning and order. Music can thank human ears for being heard; mirrors — the eyes for being reflected in them. And the world can express gratitude to human beings for simply being.

When Dostoevsky's Prince Myshkin famously proclaimed, 'beauty will save the world', he was well aware of the power of beautiful things around us to influence our being-amongst-them. Encircled by beauty, our inner being becomes beautiful. We shape our things, and they mould us in return, in a cyclical dance. By existing in this world, we first sculpt it and then rediscover ourselves within it. The world is our house that we construct and inhabit concurrently.

Considering that the word, the logos, is our world, how we wield it will determine how we build the house we live in. Jesus, as we remember, was not only the voice and the light — he was also a carpenter.

Dasein: Being Already There

Existence precedes essence.

—Sartre

Our discourse on the sequence of being reveals a logical chasm. If we search and rediscover ourselves in the present world, does that imply we somehow antecede it? It appears that there is always a 'before' concerning human existence: an ex- before -sistere; a pra- before -essentia; a pre- before -position. Where is that 'before' situated? In the 'nowhere', indeed. But not in the sense of a no-where of space, but rather in the now-here of time. At last, we discern the entity we have been searching for, the one concealed behind the mask of being and the one for whom the sun shines — as what Heidegger called *Dasein*.

The term *Dasein* (literally 'there-being') poses translation difficulties into other languages due to the peculiarity and distinctiveness of the German word *Da*, which can mean not only there but also here. Intriguingly, *Da* doesn't have to refer to space exclusively but to time as well. It can also mean then, and even more crucially: because. This simple yet ambiguous word *Da* in *Dasein* reflects the intricacy, duality, and internal contradiction of human existence. Like a candle in the dark, *Dasein* opens and *clears*[79] its world by searching and locating its position in time and space. *Dasein* is the primordial, spaceless, and timeless entity that persistently asks itself, 'where', 'when' and even 'who am I'. It is the entity donning the mask of being, the ex- and the pra- of human existence and presence in this world.

Foucault writes, 'amid all the things that are born in time and no doubt die in time, he, cut off from all origin, is already there. So that it is in him that things (those same things that hang over him) find their beginning: rather than a cut, made at some given moment in duration, he is the opening from which time in general can be reconstituted, duration can flow, and things, at the appropriate moment, can make their appearance.'[80]

The order of space versus our place within it is inverted. It is not space that is already there, but rather our *Dasein*, which is already there by searching and finding ourselves present in the container called space. Human beings already exist there before they confront and comprehend their essence. They are there, even before they situate themselves in the spatiotemporal coordinates based on the sun. If that weren't the case, the question of being where? or when? wouldn't even be questions. But they certainly are. The primordial question is, therefore, not 'where am I?' but simply 'Am I?', 'Am I present at all?' That is an even greater enigma!

The essence of space and time arises where the human already exists. 'We are this space', writes Rovelli, 'this clearing opened by the traces of memory inside the connections between our neurons. We are memory. We are nostalgia. We are longing for a future that will not come. The clearing that is opened up in this way, by memory and by anticipation, is time: a source of anguish sometimes, but in the end a tremendous gift.'[81]

We revisit the critical role of memory and our nostalgic, retrospective, and cyclical perception of the universe. Because we are already there, preceding all concepts of time and space, we are even ahead of ourselves and our personae. If we weren't running ahead of ourselves in time, we wouldn't be able to find ourselves as anything, anybody, anywhere, or anytime. There would be no such thing as 'time'. As Heidegger notes: 'We do not say: Being is, time is. We say: there is Being and there is time.' Where is this 'there'? Right there, where we are, where the is itself, is.

Religion and science concur on at least one point: they both identify an infinite space 'somewhere out there' as the origin of all space and time. Science points to the Big Bang, while religion attributes it to God in the sky. Both of these origins are perceived as far away from us. But must the origin be so distant? Why should it be located 'over there' and not 'right here', where we are: where we already know, without further inquiry, that being exists? 'It is for the gods to come to me, not for me to go to them', said Plotinus, whose 'quality of pride'

Cioran praises.[82] However, our objective isn't pride; rather, it is humble understanding.

Why do we remain discontent with our simple 'here' and seek answers about the origins of space and time in distant horizons, in Big Bangs or behind the clouds somewhere? The reason appears straightforward: we ex-sist in the world. It is in our nature to seek the origin of everything outside of ourselves. The further it is, the more attention we pay to it; the more we serve by observing it. As Bachelard puts it: 'The being-here is maintained by a being from elsewhere. Space, vast space, is the friend of being.'[83] Without the vastness of space, human existence would feel suffocating and claustrophobic. We are natural seekers of infinity. We yearn to find ourselves in an infinitely open space: boundless outer-space and infinite time. The sky is never the limit for us; it never was and never will be. We cannot even imagine ourselves without a vast open universe above and beyond. Perhaps we don't want to be the origin of space and time. As personae, we exist in a theatre of being; a theatre of vast space. As actors, our being-here depends on a distant out-there. The farther and higher that is, the better for us. Fortunately, our spaceships haven't landed on the sun yet! But would the world of the *Anthropos* truly end if they did? Does the end of the world lurk within science itself?

Jesus tells his followers, 'I am going away, and you will look for me, and you will die in your sin. Where I go, you cannot come' (John 8:21). Human existence craves the tantalizing taste of an indefinite, enigmatic infinity. Even if our spaceships one day glimpse the periphery of the cosmos, we will sustain our faith in its boundless expanses, refuting any claims of an ending. Dostoevsky rightly chastised science for pretending to provide ultimate answers to human existence. Because who said we want to find them? Who cares where the edge of the world is? The three main forces that the Grand Inquisitor identifies as captivating the human mind are authority, miracle, and, ultimately, mystery. The vast, boundless, mysterious, and infinite horizons are essential for healthy human existence. 'Nothing is more necessary to man than to bow his head in face of the infinite', Dostoevsky wrote.[84]

Standing under a star-lit night sky, gazing upon the vast open sea, the endless dense forest, or the infinitely high foggy mountains, like the protagonist in Caspar David Friedrich's famous painting, we experience the vastness of space in its most satisfying form. Yet what we feel isn't the 'there' of that vast space; what we genuinely relish is our own 'here' in relation to it.

We seek infinite space not only in the physical realm but also in the metaphysical one. Profound music offers us the vastness of space our inner souls crave. Deep poetry, literature, thoughts, and conversations all add spice to this sense of boundlessness. Even a deep, lingering gaze into a loved one's eyes can nourish us with a feeling of infinite depth. Vast space is truly a friend of being, in both outward and inward directions.

Perhaps most importantly, we find the infiniteness of space in our home: language. We may have a finite number of words at our fingertips, but we possess infinite combinations to use them. We can also invent new words and concepts through the power of our poesis. Language allows us to dwell in infinite space, exploring depths and metaphysical realms that physics cannot measure and mathematics cannot calculate. Paradoxically, a single word can encapsulate that infinity for us: the word 'there'.

The word 'there' conveys much of the vastness and boundlessness of human existence while also offering just the right touch of precision. In linguistics, 'there' is sometimes dubbed an 'existential word'; when coupled with the verb 'to be', the resulting sentence is labelled an 'existential sentence'.[85] Consider these examples:

'There has to be a solution'; 'There are good reasons why this will work out'; 'There is nothing I can do for you'; 'He is no longer there with us'; 'There is positive energy in this city'. In these instances, 'there' does not signify a specific location in space but rather a spaceless, boundless existence. We grasp the meaning without needing to inquire 'where exactly?' The word 'there' conveys abstract existence as such, simultaneously meaning 'no-where' and 'now-here'. With this power, 'there' can encompass anything in our presence; even God.

When we hear the phrase 'there is God', we don't consider a particular place where God resides. We don't concern ourselves with pinpointing exact coordinates; perhaps we don't even want to know. We simply understand that God exists 'there', in existence, somewhere we don't know. Like the light, the Word, and time, God is everywhere and nowhere. God transcends geography and astronomy, yet can be present here and now with us when we call upon Him. God is Parousia: the quintessential 'presence'. God is 'there' where we are.

'The Father and I are one' (John 10:30). That was the profound message of the Grand Inquisitor's ex-communication of Christ, who tells him: 'You have no right to add anything to what you said before.'

Clearing the Way to Being

What is the light which shines right through me and strikes my heart without hurting? It fills me with terror and burning love: with terror inasmuch as I am utterly other than it, with burning love in that I am akin to it. Wisdom, wisdom it is which shines right through me.

— Augustine

Before reaching the end of this part, let us explore one more vital aspect of the beginning: the light and its opening. The Latin word 'lumen' signifies not only 'light' but also carries a hidden meaning of 'opening of the eye'. To what? Perhaps, being?

Aside from using the term 'self' to describe ourselves, we also employ the more poetic expression of 'soul'. This soul is said to exist within us, unseen yet ever-present. The soul seems to have an independent life, separate from us, but it is also what defines our inner self. Culturally, the soul is often depicted as a non-physical substance made of pure, bright light, taking the shape of one's physical body. After death, this light departs and ascends towards the sky and the sun, where it is believed to belong.

When a child is born, we say it 'sees the light of day', as if the light were the first 'opening' or main gateway into the world. Indeed, our soul can be considered the inner light of being, the place where light occurs and being takes place. Being born, then, can be understood as giving being a place to exist in this world; to play its part in the theatre of light.

To better appreciate the significance of light, we must, once more, contrast it with darkness. Dostoevsky's Prince Myshkin does just that, recounting a friend's story moments before his supposed execution.[86] The man conveys the essence of human existence through the story, ultimately leading to the light. Before this, however, he experiences a sequence of events in his final moments, which Dostoevsky thoughtfully arranges.

Initially, the man realizes the importance of time and its boundless expansion: 'He said that those five minutes seemed to him to be a most interminable period, an enormous wealth of time; he seemed to be living, in these minutes, so many lives that there was no need as yet to think of that last moment[....]' Time, in this existential sense, stretches beyond the clock, making each last instant feel like an eternity.

Next comes the moment of confession: 'While saying good-bye to his friends he recollected asking one of them some very usual everyday question, and being much interested in the answer.' It is intriguing that the man asks and is genuinely interested in an ordinary question just before death. Rather than seeking profound answers to human existence — the God question? Is there afterlife? — the man finds solace in a simple human conversation. As Dostoevsky's genius demonstrates, the most *interesting* part is the human conversation itself, the Word, not its content.

As the man confronts the impending nothingness, he experiences a profound introspective realization of his own miraculous existence in the world:

> Then having bade farewell, he embarked upon those two minutes which he had allotted to looking into himself; he knew beforehand what he was going to think about. He wished to put it to himself as quickly and clearly as possible, that here was he, a living, thinking man, and that in three minutes he would be nobody; or if somebody or something, then what and where?

This realization highlights the mystery of his unexplained presence in the world. The phrase 'in three minutes he would be nobody; or if somebody or something, then what and where?' expresses his awareness of being a persona that still exists as someone and somewhere in this grand theatre of being. But in three minutes, he will cease to be, and nothingness will take the place of being. There will be no more 'here' or 'there', or anywhere.

Finally, the man grasps the essence of it all. In these last moments, he feels he is about to merge with pure, bright light which staggers him and steals all his attention:

A little way off there stood a church, and its gilded spire glittered in the sun. He remembered staring stubbornly at this spire, and at the rays of light sparkling from it. He could not tear his eyes from these rays of light; he got the idea that these rays were his new nature, and that in three minutes he would become one of them, amalgamated somehow with them.

The man understands that just before facing death, his soul will fully merge with the light. The opening of being and its closing are reaching their conclusion. We enter the light at birth and return to it when we die. The candlelight of being is about to be extinguished and merged with the oneness of the original void.

In ordinary language, light serves as our primary metaphor for the clearance and openness of being and everything we understand about the world. We use expressions like: 'Is this clear to you?', 'Enlighten me', 'Do you see what I mean?', 'a new theory came to light', 'she has a bright mind', 'blazing a trail', 'this is brilliant', and 'plain as daylight'. Conversely, what we don't understand is often described in terms of 'darkness': 'we were kept in the dark about this', 'her theory is obscure', 'it's all unclear to me', 'he has a shady personality' and so on.

In the realm of popular culture, ideas often materialize as light bulbs flashing above our heads, an image that aligns perfectly with the etymology of the word 'idea'. Derived from the Greek word *eidos*, which means 'visible form', the concept of 'idea' as 'form' was first developed by Plato in his *Republic*. Through this lens, the light shining upon and within us becomes the key to understanding everything, whether tangible or intangible.

Socrates, Plato's teacher, emphasized the critical role of light in comprehending the essence of things. He compared the power of sight to the sun, which illuminates objects and allows our eyes to see clearly. Drawing an intriguing parallel, he likened the soul to the eye, capable of perceiving and understanding when focused on truth and being, but forming mere *opinions* when directed towards shadows.[87] To *opine* is to *opt* for one option or another, while to *know* is to look directly at the light, the sun: the source of knowledge. Hence the *Anthropos* is the Homo sapiens, the being that knows by looking up towards the sun. He knows that the sun is *there*, and that, as Dostoevsky argued, is understanding life itself.

Socrates suggested that the sun not only brightens the external world but also illuminates our inner souls, allowing us to grasp all the phenomena we perceive as ideas. This thought is echoed in the Gospel of Matthew: 'The eye is the lamp of the body; if your eyes are healthy, your whole body will be full of light' (Matthew 6:22–24). Every idea and theory, visible or invisible, revolves around the presence of light.

Just as *eidos* waltzes with light, so too does the enchanting concept of phenomena, springing from the Greek word *phainein*, which means 'to bring to light'. The term 'phenomena' wraps its arms around everything that graces our consciousness, from the external to the internal. From 'natural phenomena' like the gust of wind, the roar of thunderstorms, and the trembling of earthquakes, to the hidden depths of our dreams, visions, ideas, imagination, insights, revelations, and inspiration, light's captivating interplay weaves the tapestry of our inner and outer worlds in the language of phenomena and ideas.

As humans, we dance with the light, entwined in an intimate duet. More profoundly still, we are the clearing — the stage on which light performs. Yet, at the heart of our being resides language, born from the word. Kierkegaard mused, 'What, then, is the voice…? Somewhere in the soul it must have a home, it has to have a birthplace.'[88] Language is our magic wand, conjuring openings and illuminating realms of light, with the word 'to be' as the most fundamental and primordial incantation.

Recall the Gospel of John, which paints a vivid picture of the relationship between the Word, being and the birth of light:

In the beginning was the Word, and the Word was with God, and the Word was God. He was with God in the beginning. Through him all things were made to be; without him nothing was made that has been made to be. In him was life, and that life was the light of all mankind. The light shines in the darkness, and the darkness has not overcome it. (John 1:1–5)

This passage narrates the dawn of being, time, and human history. Picture the instant a human being first grasped their existence, as they uttered the words 'to be', 'I am!' This marked the inception of the clearing of being, the greatest of noons, the moment we first beheld the light and discovered ourselves basking in its radiance.

In the world's light, we find truth, the unveiling of being, dazzling as it reveals its enigmatic and divine presence. Contemplate the word 'present', embracing its duality as our current moment in time and a 'gift'. Our existence becomes a cherished offering from being itself, or perhaps time. In this playful fusion of language, light, and the miracle of being, our presence twirls as both a temporal state and treasured gift.

Part III Forms of Informing

Inhabiting Worded Worlds

Speech is civilization itself ... it is silence which isolates.

—Thomas Mann

In the grand banquet of human discourse, information is a delicious dish, full of flavour and substance. Yet, we must remember that information is like a chalice, holding the wine of thought. Like a melody needing ears to dance, information seeks our minds to take form, to become an idea. In other words, information does not merely inform; it invisibly forms-in, and trans-forms.

If language is the 'house of Being', then its architecture is vital. How this house is crafted affects not only our understanding, but also our interaction with the world. We often become preoccupied with the furnishings inside, overlooking the blueprint that shapes our linguistic abode. It is the house that we inhabit which is the most difficult to examine while we're in it.

In this last part, we'll explore the art of language, delving into its oral and written forms, along with their digital offspring. To set the stage, let's recall language's *raison d'être*: shared understanding. For language to thrive, it must be a symphony, resonating in harmony with all listeners. Words are like the colourful notes of this symphony: abbreviations, signs, and metaphors representing our world's wonders.

The Ancient Greeks recognized the power of symbols, or *symbolon*, things 'thrown together'. Thrown, because of the need to agree quickly on symbols and signs, emphasizing speed. Rapid communication is crucial for uniting people under a common language. 'The history of language', says Nietzsche, 'is the history of a process of abbreviation; based on this quick comprehension people always unite closer and closer. The greater the danger, the greater is the need of agreeing quickly and readily about what is necessary.'[1] We can build roads, bridges, cities, and republics because we can quickly agree on what we communicate and share. As finite beings with limited time, we cannot delve into the depths of every word, for that would, indeed, take too much time.

Language is primarily intended for communication, not analysis. If the world were composed solely of linguists, philologists, and philosophers, progress might stall as we'd be preoccupied with examining language instead of living and creating. This idea is exemplified by the symbolic meaning behind Socrates' condemnation to death by the Athenian public. Philosophers tend to endlessly question words and concepts without providing satisfying, firm answers. While their role in the pursuit of truth is undeniably valuable, they can also hinder quick consensus and are seen as outsiders, even *idiots*.[2]

Efficient communication depends on the use of comprehensible, accessible, and memorable verbal and non-verbal symbols. Communication flourishes when signs are widely shared and mutually accepted. Conversely, a difficult language hinders communication and stifles the sharing of ideas and things.

A key goal of language is to facilitate understanding, a process often aided by efficient and clear communication. When we use simple words like 'table', 'democracy', or 'love', we convey similar ideas to listeners.[3] The mere sound of these words immediately triggers imaginative connotations in our neurons about what is being said, and the lightbulb turns on.

The captivating power of spoken communication lies in its instantaneous nature, as we first learn language through listening before reading. Emphasizing this potency, the phrase 'hearing is obeying' captures the undeniable impact of oral communication. When words are spoken, we're swept up in the moment, with little chance to reflect or react, making our responses deeply influenced. Thus, the compelling role of speed in communication underscores the unmatched importance of the spoken word.

Nietzsche, the philosopher-poet, lamented the loss of dynamism in written thoughts compared to the vivacity of speech. Written words, once thorny and spicy, he bemoaned, now risk turning stale and tedious.[4]

Enter the symphony of sound, the pulsating power of music, and watch as it captivates our senses. We dance, surrendering to the rhythm, our bodies liberated from our minds, momentarily losing control. In this shared, spaceless existence, the acoustic allure of language weaves its spell, uniting us all.

Spoken words, with their hypnotic charm, not only bewitch listeners but also those who breathe life into them. The ancient Greeks, reciting Homeric epics, immersed in their own tales, stepped into an ecstatic trance called *mimesis*.[5] Stories transformed into theatre as they were spoken out loud, and the bard's influence grew so potent that Plato, the rationalist, sought to banish Homer and Hesiod from his Republic. When Plato's ideas crystallized into visible, static forms, they invited analysis, heralding the dawn of re-flection and rationality. So, Plato emerged as the progenitor of contemplation by building the first ever abstract temple, the *eidos*.

Plato knew that the sound's bewitching power orchestrates grand symphonies, where crowds submerge in the harmonious melodies of music or the magnetic pull of eloquent speeches — the enemy of analysis. Spoken words, serenading our ears, evoke Chekhov's comparison between living talk as song and books as printed scores.[6] When words waltz from voice to paper, the rhythm transforms and solidifies into a static, tangible temple, the written page.

In contrast to speaking, reading is a solitary activity, offering privacy and bringing forth one's inner voice. Early readers, captivated by words, couldn't help but read aloud. In the fifth century, Augustine marvelled at his mentor St

Ambrose, who miraculously read to himself: 'now, as he read, his eyes glanced over the pages and his heart searched out the sense, but his voice and tongue were silent.'[7] Silent reading was a novelty then, and centuries would pass before it became second nature.

The verb 'to read' hailing from Old English *redan*, means 'advise', 'counsel', and 'put in order'. Reading, as delayed speech, grants time for thoughts to arrange and self-counsel. Consider Aristotle, Plato's renowned student and advisor to Alexander the Great. His first gift to young Alexander: the skill of reading. As Neil Postman puts it, writing transforms speech, giving rise to various disciplines: 'the grammarian, the logician, the rhetorician, the historian, the scientist — all those who must hold language before them so that they can see what it means, where it errs, and where it is leading.'[8] As a reader, seeing words before you enables the construction of complex ideas, like building a temple of thought. These mental bricks, written words, lay the foundation for grander concepts. Reading eyes navigate the temple with ease, while listening ears struggle to grasp fleeting 'winged words' as Homer called them.

Without the written word, abstract notions like 'democracy', 'freedom', or 'justice' would wane across history. Etchings on paper are history's very essence, preserved not just momentarily, as in Homeric tales, but eternally, echoing Plato's unyielding *eidos*.

A Written Scenario

For us, 'literacy' has carried a weight of implication, an extension far beyond any technical definition. Ours have been, above all else, civilizations and communities of the word; sentences found and inhabit our cities.

—George Steiner

Our phonetic alphabet, based on phonemes or sounds, turns spoken words into static, silent forms. Written language is speech transformed; for instance, Plato's writings echo Socrates' spoken words, never penned by Socrates himself. Reading, then, is secretly listening without hearing. Literacy extends speech and language into silent realms, still adhering to synchronization and linguistic laws.

The invisible 'council of things' shapes agreements in oral speech, following its unique set of rules. Written language turns these abstract agreements into tangible, touchable documents such as constitutions vital to our republics, laws, and social systems.[9] Ideas unite the public, and the stronger the unity, the more developed the means of discussing them.

Before widespread literacy, public unity emerged in oral societies like Homeric Greece through gatherings in theatres or agoras. Plato envisioned an ideal Greek city, where all could hear a single public orator (around 5000 people), sound as the chief communication technology. In European cities during the Middle Ages, according to Lewis Mumford's *The City in History*, bell towers supplanted the orator's voice, with the city's borders contained within the belfries' reach. In both instances, the scope of unity relied on sound.[10]

Yet, for vast geographical areas, direct speech was insufficient, prompting the need for paper and papyrus. Harold Innis asserts that the Roman Empire's bureaucratic development hinged on papyrus supplies for far-reaching administration. While the emperor could address the population through direct speech, maintaining a vast empire required a unified communication network. Papyrus became the veins connecting the entire system. Innis even links Rome's fall to dwindling papyrus supplies from Egypt, eventually lost to external invasions.[11]

Humboldt suggests 'civilization' arises when societies across extensive territories share the same communication media, fostering connection and coordination. He observes that the

Greeks and Romans fell short in this regard due to limited availability of external media for international communication and the state of civilization at the time.[12] 'Civilization' embodies the idea of the city (*civita*) extending across vast territories, achievable only through communication methods transcending the immediate present.

Before literacy, entities like Greece, Germany, Italy, or Europe as we know today didn't exist. Writing enabled communication across vast regions, laying groundwork for republics, states, nations, and empires. In the fifteenth century, Gutenberg's printing technology catalysed the emergence of European national languages and nation-states. Print let individuals not just to obey their vernaculars aurally, but to visualize, analyse and document them, creating national unity within their bounds.[13] In a way, written language on paper served as a precursor to envisioning one's country on a map.

Over centuries, printing technology embedded language in national consciousness, surpassing city-state boundaries. Gutenberg's press led to language standardization and adherence to writing rules, subtly introducing the rule of law. Walter Ong notes that print-based communication required uniform writing, merging regional dialects into a single, national 'correct' language.[14] This grapholect manifested spoken dialects in graphic form through written words, compelling people to obey written over spoken language.

For instance, the German language, noted for its structured grammar and syntax, was shaped by writing standardization, as Nietzsche observed. He notes, 'Gradually people came to this conclusion, and spoke even as they wrote.'[15] The rise of literary style over spoken was evident, with shared affectation and ostentation underpinning a common language. Humboldt called this phenomenon 'phonetic decay', occurring in Germany at literacy's peak.[16]

But writing's impact on spoken language didn't stop at Germany; it rippled across Western Europe. Derrida, channelling Rousseau, claims writing imposed a 'tyranny' on people, altering how they spoke and spelled French words.[17] This phenomenon thrived in highly literary languages, where written texts played a starring role.

The 'man of letters' became a figure of admiration. In the Middle Ages, as Michael Pye notes in the *Edge of the World*, 'the ability to write, not just read, was still a matter of privilege, something you often paid someone else to do properly. Anything written had an almost magical quality; it became more right, more real and always more essential than anything a live witness could say.'[18] When Dostoevsky's Myshkin travels from Switzerland to his distant family in Russia, he faces the threat of rejection. Yet, one particular skill saves Myshkin: calligraphy. This artful penmanship was the solitary practical skill he possessed, allowing Myshkin to earn a living and secure a place among his kin. The Idiot was a man of letters in the direct sense of the word.

'Literally true', we still say, valuing written words above spoken. As *mythos* (spoken word) transformed into 'myth', legends[19] gained more credibility. Eventually Western culture came to favour the 'legendary' over the 'mythical'.

Foucault asserts that the Renaissance period, marked by the advent of printing and Oriental manuscripts, sparked a revolution in Western culture that prioritized writing over oral traditions. This shift allowed for a deeper interpretation of religious texts, highlighting the written word as the essence of language.[20] Organized and cooperative information sharing bloomed. Modern Western laws, constitutions, and contracts hinge on the rule of law, prioritizing written words over spoken. In literate societies, written rules are followed more closely. The law (*lex*) governs because it is read (*legere*) on paper.

Here, the written word takes on an almost sacred quality. For example, in the United States, the Constitution is revered as almost a divine document. Democracy, the rule of law, and the free-market system would be impossible without the dominance of literacy. McLuhan explains that without the uniform processing facilitated by literacy, centralized national groupings and market systems could not exist.[21]

Come the sixteenth century, money distanced itself from gold as trust in the written word swelled.[22] Money evolved into an abstract concept based on trust, with literacy empowering trust to become the new gold. In *The Merchant of Venice*, Shakespeare explores the metaphor of written agreements and their tangible monetary consequences. Shylock, a moneylender, demands a pound of flesh from the merchant Antonio, who defaulted on his loan. Antonio's agreement to this outlandish condition reveals the power and reality of the written word.

When Bassanio presents the letter to Portia, he describes it as follows:

> Here is a letter, lady,
> The paper as the body of my friend,
> And every word in it a gaping wound
> Issuing life blood.

The play spotlights the literal embodiment of law on paper, which we now recognize as a 'corporation'. The written word became not just information, but incorporation.

The printing press ushered in decentralization as well. Standardized print managed trade and legal matters, liberating cities from orators and the church. Independent courts emerged, handling written affairs and promoting decentralization. Literacy transformed society, steering it away from oral dictates. Derrida observes that 'the modern capital is always a monopoly of writing'.[23] The US Constitution's First Amendment, 'freedom of the press', highlights the printing press's significance. Initially, 'press' denoted the printing press itself, with newspapers emerging later. The written word became essential for governance, unlocking new democratic possibilities. Literacy was therefore the antidote to dictatorship in the most literal sense of the word.

The Great Schism

The printed word democratized religion, enabling the individual to confront the Bible directly, without priestly intervention.

—McLuhan

This monumental shift from oral to written communication, which left no aspect of European social life untouched, including religion, was also reflected in the arts of the time. Adriaen van de Venne's 1614 painting 'Fishing for Souls' serves as a striking visual allegory of the early form of information warfare between the written and the spoken word.

Van de Venne's painting features a river with two banks, with Protestants on the left and Catholics on the right. In the centre, Catholic and Protestant boats fish for lost souls. The Protestant boat is filled with Luther's theses and spare books, ready for those who will join them. In contrast, the Catholic boat has books only held by choir boys singing the gospels out loud. The Protestants cast a net containing books for the literate souls who want to join them. Catholics, on the other hand, forcefully grab the souls from the water.

Van de Venne's portrayal reveals a subtle bias towards the Protestants, as evidenced by the sun shining on the Protestant side of the river. Despite this bias, the painting captures the essence of the era, depicting how souls were won using different tools and methods: an early form of information warfare.

The decentralization of faith and the rise of literacy in Europe following Gutenberg's invention set the stage for a new era. People began to interpret divine words on their own, no longer solely relying on priests. In doing so, they were embracing the written word, reshaping the way they experienced faith and engaging with religion in a more personal way.

The Protestant Reformation, which challenged the Catholic Church's dominance, can be traced back to the transformative shift in communication and the rise of literacy across Europe following Gutenberg's invention. With the printing press making written texts more accessible, Protestantism rapidly gained ground in Germany and Northern Europe — areas where literacy had the most significant impact.[24] As Nietzsche noted, 'The German does not read aloud, he does not read for the ear, but only with his eyes; he has put his ears away in the drawer for the time.'[25] In this new era, the revolution of faith emerged in tandem with the Gutenberg communication revolution.

Martin Luther's written theses spread like wildfire. Walter Ong, a Protestant priest, observed that, 'Almost every literate Puritan kept some sort of journal', adding that 'The advent of print intensified the inwardness fostered by script. The age of print was immediately marked in Protestant circles by advocacy of private, individual interpretation of the Bible.'[26]

As a result, people began to read the Bible privately at home, no longer needing to hear God's voice through church sermons. They interpreted the divine words individually and adapted them to their daily lives through exegesis. Thus, Protestants transformed from *hearers* of priests to independent interpreters, readers, of the Bible, living up to their name as they disobeyed, protested against the established religious order. An order which was hitherto based on sound.

Nietzsche further explained that 'Luther made the Scriptures available to everyone', which ultimately led to their interpretation by philologists, who he deemed 'the annihilators of every faith based upon books'.[27] Among these philologists were Nietzsche himself and Friedrich Schleiermacher, a German Protestant theologian who founded the philosophical school of Hermeneutics, dedicated to interpreting biblical, philosophical, and literary texts.

The divergence in the Christian faith can also be linked to etymological distinctions. Protestantism, often referred to as Evangelical, is based on the Gospel (Evangelie), the holy book. Catholicism, conversely, means 'all-embracing', subject to a single, comprehensive authority: the Vatican. Unlike Protestantism, Catholicism revolves around a specific location and spokesperson for the divine Word: the pope. The Vatican serves as a unifying institution in Catholicism, adhering to the principles of centralized communication from a single source. Just as the church in the main market square of many European towns, the Vatican communicates with Catholics worldwide, with the pope as the leading orator.

In contrast, Protestantism moves away from a centralized location. Their source of God's voice is not the church, but the book, accessible individually at home. With its basis in the book, Protestantism transforms every home into a church and every church into a home. Among the three major Abrahamic religions, Protestantism stands out as having no designated physical, centralized location on earth. It lacks a Vatican (Catholicism), Mecca (Islam), Jerusalem (Judaism), or Mount Athos (Greek Orthodoxy). In Protestantism, God is reached directly through the book, making Him simultaneously elusive and ever-present, embodied within the written word itself.

Dostoevsky, an Orthodox Christian, expressed concern about the Protestant separation from its Roman Catholic base. His Grand Inquisitor comments on humanity's rebellion against divine authority, suggesting that such revolt is temporary and will come at a considerable cost. However, even Dostoevsky believed that God should not be blindly obeyed, but sought through one's actions and judgements. Father Zosima, a character in his novel, symbolically instructs the young monk Alyosha Karamazov to leave the church and independently search for his life path.

Additionally, the Grand Inquisitor's rejection of Christ's appearance on earth represents a denial of God's absolute and undisputed physical presence *somewhere*. Unlike Jesus, God is not the word made flesh; He does not have a body and should never be embodied. He exists in the word itself.

Twilight of the Electric Sun

I change too quickly: my today refutes my yesterday. When I ascend I often jump over steps, and no step forgives me that.

—Nietzsche

Technology has emerged as our novel faith, binding us in ways unparalleled by any other force. It is not worship that defines this devotion, but the connections forged, eradicating distances, and ushering us into temporal and spatial intimacy. Electric tendrils, wired and wireless, weave an omnipresent sun of our own making. As McLuhan observed, in the electric age 'you are not going anywhere, because you are always already there'. This sentiment rings truest in the internet's realm, where we are perpetually present in the virtual world, a situation we can call the instant.

From earth (*humus*) sprouted *Homo*, the human, yet in the electric age, we find ourselves unmoored, straddling an electric *nubes*, the cloud. This nebulous habitat embodies a utopian, placeless world. Here, we don another guise, the digital persona, adding further complexity to our already intricate existential identities. Little wonder that identity crises emerge in our technological epoch, as we grapple with the management of multiple masks. Our digital era could be anointed Raskolnikov 2.0: a dual cleavage and fragmentation within oneself; one aspect dwelling on the cloud, the other tethered to earth.

As expounded in this text, language remains the paramount medium for situating ourselves within the world. It moulds our past, future, and above all, our present, shaping our perceptions of time and even space. Beyond communication's content, the manner in which we access information wields considerable power. The velocity and abundance of words we navigate daily significantly impact our experiences in the world of words. Inevitably, the shape of information morphs its substance: our very essence.

Hartmut Rosa, in *Social Acceleration*, suggests that 'depression can doubtless be conceived as a pathology of time'.[28] Time, the central edifice of being and memory, bears the brunt of our electric age's assault — by now a staggering 8 billion instances of it. The so-called age of anxiety emerges from this temporal pathology and accelerated metamorphosis, a relentless whirlwind of transformation. The electric sun bathes the world in unison, melding our global presence. Crisis, identity, and time intertwine. The sheer multitude of choices (*krisis*) demanded within fleeting moments renders the maintenance of a stable identity (*idem*) a Herculean feat.

In our electrifying era, we dance to the rhythm of rapid communication and elevated speeds: savouring fast food, racing in fast cars, surfing the fast internet, mastering speed reading, embracing speed learning, and engaging in speed dating. We surf, skim, scroll, snap, and swipe with zest. We live exuberantly, savouring each fleeting moment, ensuring everything is current and up to date. Our economies flourish on 'just-in-time' principles, 'moving fast and breaking things'. We eagerly seek to be 'frontrunners', all the while encouraging those who might be lagging behind. In this dynamic world, novelty is ever-refreshing, and we eagerly reach for the future.

We find ourselves immersed in the modern world, where the past is but a distant memory, and our eyes are set on the horizon of progress. Fear of being left behind fuels our drive to draw the future ever closer, and in this age of instant gratification, all converges into a vibrant *hic et nunc* (here and now).

Being 'modern' is akin to living in the present moment,[29] and much like fashion (*la mode* in French), modernity is a delightful trend to embrace. At its core, modernity dances to the beat of change, letting go of the past, and pursuing the new with vigour. As we waltz through modernity, we remain contemporary and relevant. After all, who would want to be outdated or old-fashioned? Modernity resonates with youth, vitality, and energy, qualities that paint a vivid and desirable portrait of our present moment.

Yet, in the midst of our revolutions and ambitions, we often find ourselves spinning in circles. As Luhmann aptly suggests in *Observations on Modernity*, society tries to 'solve the problems of self-description by means of a time-line, "It barely understands itself, and so it marks its newness by relegating the old, thereby covering up its own embarrassment at not really knowing what is going on"'.[30] What is actually going on in modernity? *Everything, Everywhere and All at Once*. The whirlwind of modernization and acceleration of communication have become an entrancing dance; the more words we generate, the more our understanding spins. The search for meaning and understanding seems to grow alongside the hunger for more words, but neither is fully sated. 'We live in a world where there is more and more information, and less and less meaning',[31] writes Jean Baudrillard, whose book *Simulacra and Simulation* inspired *The Matrix*.

In this grand ball of modernity, we're invited to consider Jacques Ellul's concept of 'the humiliation of the word', a reminder of the importance of the word itself. As we seek meaning through an ever-growing sea of words as mere information, let us not forget their aesthetic and formative value. In our world of abundant and artfully crafted language, the techno-logos, the value of the word vanishes before us.

In the Elizabethan epoch, the printing press and written word emerged as novel technologies, stirring the imagination. Shakespeare, with a touch of jest, lamented the printed book for provoking a voracious appetite for new, trivial, and vacuous 'words, words, words'. The Bard's joyful dialogue in Hamlet captures this sentiment:

> Polonius: What do you read, my lord?
> Hamlet: Words, words, words.
> Polonius: What is the matter, my lord?
> Hamlet: Between who?
> Polonius: I mean, the matter that you read, my lord.

As books were deemed machines for frivolous words in Shakespeare's era, newspapers faced Nietzsche's scrutiny centuries later. The philosopher quipped that newspapers merely satisfied the curiosity of the 'history-hungry'. In Nietzsche's words, 'The war has not yet ended, and already it is transformed on printed paper a hundred thousand times over; soon it will be promoted as the newest stimulant for the palate of those greedy for history.'[32]

The Western world saw the swift and concise newspaper begin to outpace the book. Innis cites French author Alphonse de Lamartine, who, in 1831, declared that the book arrived too late and the only book possible in his day was the newspaper.[33] As the proliferation of newspapers accelerated, Gustave Le Bon observed that opinions became ephemeral, never gaining traction or widespread acceptance.[34] Adding to this, for Steiner journalistic presentation fostered a temporality of equal instantaneity, with all things being only daily and quickly 'remaindered'.[35]

The etymology of 'journal' and 'journalism' traces back to the French word *jour* (day), signifying a daily exploration of information, a continual turning of events, a persistent *katastrophe*. Our era has transcended newspapers, adopting what we now call newsfeeds: a testament to our insatiable hunger for more words. These feeds do not offer conclusions or understanding but are engineered for constant refreshing and endless revolutions. We are nourished by news, not merely daily, but hourly and by the minute.

Our age distinguishes itself from the past written age as not merely fast-paced, but instant. The electric sun illuminates the entire globe concurrently, day and night. And while Plato's acoustic city thrived with 5000 people, the internet now serves as an online agora for 8 billion participants, dancing in a whirlwind of words and ideas.

Electronica Vulgaris

The clearest way to see through a culture is to attend to its tools for conversation.

—Neil Postman

Within his memoirs, German-Jewish philologist Victor Klemperer documented an aspect largely overlooked by others in his era: the subtle, systematic, and swift debasement of his mother tongue. This decline would eventually bear severe consequences, not only for Klemperer's native Germany but for the entire world. To evade potential persecution, he concealed his memoirs under the code name LTI, or *Lingua Tertii Imperii: The Language of The Third Reich*.

'Language does not merely write and think for me', he penned, 'it also increasingly dictates my feelings and governs my entire spiritual being the more unquestioningly I abandon myself to it.'[36] Klemperer argued that the mechanization and dehumanization of life in Nazi Germany primarily resulted from the language's dehumanization under Nazi rule. 'The most potent influence was exerted neither by individual speeches nor by articles or flyers, posters or flags; it was not achieved by things which one had to absorb by conscious thought or conscious emotions. Instead, Nazism infiltrated the flesh and blood of the people through single words, idioms, and sentence structures imposed on them in a million repetitions and adopted mechanically and unconsciously.'

Klemperer provides myriad examples of this transition as he observed the systematic mechanization and dehumanization of the German of Goethe and Schiller, occurring on an annual, monthly, and even weekly basis. Ordinary German words, like *ewigkeit* (eternity) or *aufziehen* (wind up), were persistently overemphasized and employed in increasingly unconventional contexts. Simultaneously, others such as *gleichhalten* (to force into line) or *voll ausgelastet* (working at full capacity) were novel terms coined by the regime itself.

The Nazis' mere misapplication of words, distortion, and utilization in entirely foreign contexts led an entire nation to unconsciously follow suit. The initial *blitzkriegs* (lightning wars) occurred domestically, with the German people as the first victims. Such verbal blitzkriegs were made possible by the emerging instant communication technology of Klemperer's time: the radio. With the radio, the German ear was exposed. In a Nazi party conference speech, Joseph Goebbels concedes, 'It is no exaggeration to say that the German revolution, at least in the form it took, would have been impossible without the airplane and the radio.'[37] The radio in Nazi Germany even bore a welcoming, unifying, and community-like moniker, *Volksempfänger* ('the people's receiver'). The German people, even beyond their nation's borders, were united in one location. And that place was not terrestrial, but 'on air'.

Klemperer observed that, owing to radio, LTI introduced a previously unknown phenomenon in Germany: the elimination of any distinction between spoken and written language. This development contravened the trend Nietzsche discerned when Germany experienced a rise in spoken literary style. While aware of the inherent German mistrust of the spoken word, Klemperer noted that radio, in the hands of the Nazis, inclined its language to be emotionally shouted rather than conveyed by the linear argumentation demanded in a literate environment.[38] The Führer embodied this approach with exceptional skill: the dictator who commanded obedience because he was heard loud and clear in every ear his voice could reach.

As we venture into the digital era, our focus shifts from LTI to LQI (*Langue Quotidienne Informatisée*), French for 'computerized daily language'. French psychoanalyst Yann Diener walks in Klemperer's footsteps, observing the increasingly technologized language of our technological times. Nowadays, we discuss 'exchanging data', 'browsing through the grocery store' and employ terms like life-hacks, bio-hacks, foodporn, and burnout. We plug in, log off, tune in, and get turned on. We no longer simply call ourselves by names but identify our personae as distinct identities. Diener remarks that LQI increasingly governs our sexuality, too: we refer to 'binary' and 'non-binary' sexual identities as if humans were reduced to mere 1s and 0s.[39] Are we already immersed in *The Matrix*?

In the 1999 cult film, the main characters adopt binary codes. The hero, Neo, is the anagram for 'the One', number one. His girlfriend, Trinity, represents the number three. The deceitful Cypher symbolizes 'number' or 'algorithm'. Morpheus, who presents Neo with the choice between the red and blue pills, shares his name with the Greek god of sleep. In *The Matrix*, Neo is uncertain if his life is real or merely a dream. We sometimes share his doubt. Elon Musk, perhaps our time's most respected entrepreneur and technological visionary, speculates that we may inhabit a computer simulation. Indeed, we navigate a simulated world of simultaneity; *simul* meaning 'together' or 'at once'. Our digital epoch, marked by rapid transformations, morphs the very thingness of our shared reality into an elusive no-thingness, slipping through our grasp.

Surprisingly, the idea of a universe governed by numbers has ancient roots. Long before Musk's speculations, Pythagoras proposed a cosmos ruled by divine numerals. The father of geometry and mathematics also founded Pythagoreanism, a religion characterized by peculiar rules, as Bertrand Russell describes. From abstaining from beans to avoiding mirrors in the presence of light, numbers held sway in guiding adherents through existence. The eternal abstraction of numbers, intertwined with a yearning to control reality, has been a recurring theme throughout human history. Pythagoras' mathematical mysticism 'has been both profound and unfortunate', Russel concludes.

The Bible, too, is embroidered with numerals: the Holy Trinity, Ten Commandments, Twelve Apostles, forty days and nights, and so forth. Numbers have long been entwined with the human psyche, and this relationship endures. The Book of Revelation attributes a number even to the Devil: the notorious 666. The text hints at a profound truth: 'Here is wisdom. He that hath understanding, let him count the number of the beast; for it is the number of a man: and his number is Six hundred and sixty and six' (Revelation 13:18). Numbers are for those who 'hath understanding'; those who can perceive the world, even the Devil, through numerals. However, the number belongs not to the beast, it is emphasized, but to man.

Michael Pye recounts a tale from the 1330s, when Parisian theologians began to quantify sins and indulgences mathematically. Virtue and vice, endowed with numeric weight, emerged when the pope set a price on penance. 'When both virtue and sin can be turned into numbers, and calculated and assessed, mathematics has entered the minds of theologians and philosophers and not just engineers and merchants', Pye observes.

And yet, numbers, like words, are mere metaphors, offspring of the human mind yearning for order.[40] They spring from our earliest tools for digital computation: our fingers (*digitus*). Our existence goes beyond numbers, for life is not a cold calculation but a symphony of words, a pulsating melody that predates both the sacred and the profane. We live and think through dynamic, temporal verbs, not static digits. We don't say we re-count being; we re-call it. The rhythm of being isn't computed, it is savoured, and swayed to. It bears no correct solution, but only the resonance of truth.

Notes

Part I Through the Persona

1. *Ex* means 'out of' or 'forth'.
2. The term 'barbarian' was invented in Ancient Greece, and was first used to describe Persians and Phoenicians who made unintelligible sounds to them (blah blah — bar bar).
3. Harari, *Sapiens*, 41–43.
4. Everett, *How Language Began*, 3–4.
5. Gadamer, *Philosophical Hermeneutics*, 65.
6. Humboldt, *Linguistic Variability*, 2.
7. Foucault, *The Order of Things*, 325.
8. Merleau-Ponty, *Consciousness and the Acquisition of Language (Studies in Phenomenology and Existential Philosophy)*, 75.
9. Heidegger, *What Is Called Thinking?*, 123.
10. Wittgenstein, *Philosophical Investigations*, 109.
11. Humboldt, *Linguistic Variability*, 74.
12. Steiner, *After Babel*, 133.
13. McLuhan, *Laws of Media*, 121.
14. Sex is a 'profoundly semantic act', says Steiner in *After Babel*. 'To speak and to make love is to enact a distinctive twofold universality; both forms of communication are universals of human physiology as well as of social evolution.'
15. Luhmann, *Love as Passion: The Codification of Intimacy*, 22.
16. Tolstoy, *War and Peace*, bk. 3 Chapter 2.
17. Only later in the book does the enigmatic episode reveal itself. Tolstoy explains that Pierre was not true to himself when uttering those words. His marriage to Helene ultimately becomes unhappy. When Bezukhov ends up a prisoner of war in a French camp, he realizes that he had not been free when declaring his 'love' for Helene. Instead, he was merely following the established norms and codes of conduct within his social circle. Even in making such

a crucial decision as marriage, his initiative was absent, and he remained ensnared by the medium of love's linguistic code.

18. See Everett, *How Language Began*.

19. Cioran, *Anathemas and Admirations*.

20. Heidegger, *Poetry, Language, Thought*, 129.

21. In both of these ancient languages, the semantics of the verb 'to hear' — *hupakouo* in Greek, and *shema* in Hebrew — involve a kind of hearing that includes obedience or action in response to what is heard. They both call for more than just physical hearing, they call for understanding and response.

22. *Hieran* in Old English means 'to hear' as well as 'to obey'. In Romance languages, to hear (*écouter, escuchar, ascoltare*) all come from the Latin *auscolto* which means both 'to hear' as well as 'to obey'. The Russian *slushat'* (to listen) is almost synonymous with *slushat'sya* (to obey). In German, *Hören* (to hear) is present in *Gehören* (to belong) and *Gehorchen* (to obey). In Dutch, 'to obey' (*Gehoorzamen*) would even translate as 'hearing together'.

23. Pascal, *Pensées*, 63.

24. Nietzsche, *Human all Too Human*.

25. Dostoevsky, *The Idiot*.

26. Levi-Strauss, *Wild Thought*, 106.

27. Cioran, *Anathemas and Admirations*

28. Pierre Hadot's wonderful book *The Veil of Isis* explores this theme thoroughly.

29. Nietzsche, *The Joyous Science*, 23.

30. Aristotle, *Metaphysics*, 32.

31. Aristotle, 115.

32. Merleau-Ponty, *Consciousness and the Acquisition of Language (Studies in Phenomenology and Existential Philosophy)*, 6.

33. Foucault, *The Order of Things*, 104.

34. Moro, *A Brief History of the Verb To Be*.

35. Nietzsche, *Human all too Human.*

36. Heidegger, *History of the Concept of Time,* 56.

37. Everett, *Don't Sleep There Are Snakes,* 211.

38. Quoted by Pascal in *Pensées.*

39. Gadamer, *Philosophical Hermeneutics,* 71.

40. Steiner, *After Babel,* 221.

41. Heidegger, *Poetry, Language, Thought.* 174.

42. Augustine, *The Confessions,* Book X.

43. Augustine, *The Confessions,* Book X (31)

44. Bachelard, *Intuition of the Instant.*

45. Kierkegaard, *Either/Or,* 50.

46. Cioran, *Anathemas and Admirations.*

47. Nietzsche, *Beyond Good and Evil.*

48. Dante Aligheri, *The Divine Comedy, Purgatorio,* Canto 33.

49. Kahneman, *Thinking, Fast and Slow,* 381.

50. Sartre, *Nausea,* 36.

51. Dostoevsky, *The Idiot,* pt. 1 II.

52. Levi-Strauss, *Wild Thought,* 114.

53. Ellul, *Humiliation of the Word,* 37.

54. Steiner, *After Babel.*

55. Dostoevsky, *The Gambler,* chap. XIII.

56. Dostoevsky, *Crime and Punishment,* Epilogue II.

57. As described by Dostoevsky himself in a letter.

58. Levi-Strauss, *Wild Thought,* 303.

59. The Economist, *The world's most valuable resource is no longer oil, but data,* May 6, 2017.

60. The word 'technology' consists of two Greek words *tekhne* ('to craft') and *logos* ('language').

61. 'Did God, asks Jewish folklore, not invent man so that He might hear him tell tales?' (Steiner)

62. Steiner writes: 'there is no temporal singularity, no enigma of historicity ('why in this one place, why at that one time?') in the Judaic sense of the Creation and of the Mosaic reception and transmission of the Law. There is

a strict, utterly mysterious temporality in the coming and ministry of Christ. [...] The Torah is indeterminately synchronic with all individual and communal life. The Gospels, Epistles and Acts are not.'

63. The Greek concept *historia* means 'investigation'.
64. Wittgenstein, *Philosophical Investigations*, 81.
65. Havelock, *Preface to Plato*, 61–86.
66. Aristotle, *Poetics*, 42.
67. Nietzsche, *The Joyous Science*, 180.
68. Bachelard, *The Poetics of Space*.
69. Steiner, *After Babel*.
70. Plato, *Republic*, 37.
71. Humboldt, *Linguistic Variability*, 149.
72. Merleau-Ponty quotes German language theorist Karl Bühler, who found that children adopt the 'accent' of their first language even before they start speaking it: 'Bühler, in his "theory of language", has observed that German children initially place the tonic accent on the second syllable of their vocal utterances, but quickly shift it to the first syllable. They take on, as it were, "the German accent". Thus, even before speaking, the child appropriates the rhythm and stress (accentuation) of his own language.'
73. Stefan Zweig, *The World of Yesterday*.

Part II Where Is Time?

1. Buonomano, *Your Brain Is a Time Machine*, 57.
2. Dostoevsky, *The Idiot*.
3. Aristotle, *On Memory and Recollection*.
4. Steiner, *After Babel*, 136.
5. See Buonomano, *Your Brain Is a Time Machine*.
6. Steiner, *After Babel*, 165.
7. Steiner, *After Babel*, 138.
8. Translated from Romanian by A.Z Foreman.
9. Cioran, *Anathemas and Admirations*. 12

10. Homer says Odysseus is called 'the Son of Pain': 'a name he'll earn in full' (bk. 19 460–464).
11. Stanford University, 'Text of Steve Jobs' Commencement Address (2005).'
12. Nietzsche, *Thus Spoke Zarathustra*, 121.
13. Kierkegaard, *Either/Or*, 43.
14. The owl (called *Athene noctua*) is the symbol of wisdom because it is a bird that sees in the darkness of the night.
15. Rilke, *Letters to a Young Poet*, Letter 8.
16. Sartre, *Nausea*.
17. Kierkegaard, *Either/Or*, 46.
18. Kahneman, *Thinking, Fast and Slow*, 67.
19. Augustine, *The Confessions*, Book VII, (8).
20. Steiner, *Real Presences*.
21. Luhmann, *Observations on Modernity*, 78.
22. In the *Poetics*, Aristotle writes: 'The poet and the historian differ not by writing in verse or in prose. The work of Herodotus might be put into verse, and it would still be a species of history, with metre (rhythm) no less than without it. The true difference is that one relates what has happened, the other what may happen. Poetry, therefore, is a more philosophical and a higher thing than history: for poetry tends to express the universal, history the particular. By the universal I mean how a person of a certain type will on occasion speak or act, according to the law of probability or necessity; and it is this universality at which poetry aims in the names she attaches to the personages. The particular is, for example, what Alcibiades did or suffered...'
23. See Isaiah Berlin's *The Hedgehog and the Fox*
24. Heidegger, *Poetry, Language, Thought*, 139.
25. Luhmann, *Observations on Modernity*, 94.
26. Dostoyevsky, *The Brothers Karamazov*, The Grand Inquisitor.
27. Kolakowski, *Is God Happy? Selected Essays*.

28. Some languages give us further hints that confirm this priority of the present time. In Spanish, the word for 'never' is *nunca* which we can interpret to mean not now. The message given by this Spanish word is that what is not now — isn't; it simply doesn't exist. Similarly, in Russian, the word for 'the present' (*nastoyasheye*) is the same word for 'real', 'true' and 'genuine'.

29. Kierkegaard, *Either/Or*, 79.

30. For instance, *estar* in Spanish, *être* in *French*, *yest'* in Russian, *ist* in German, and *is* in English. All owe their etymology to Latin, where 'that is' translates to *hoc est* with *est* representing *stare*: to stand.

31. 'As he finished, Joachim would return, and it might be as late as half past two before the latter went into his loggia, and the hush of the main rest period fell upon the Berghof. Not quite, perhaps; perhaps it would be nearer the truth to call it a quarter after, but these odd quarter-hours outside the round figures do not count, they are swallowed up unregarded, in places where one reckons time in large units — on long train journeys of many hours on end, or wherever one is in a state of vacant suspense, with all one's being concentrated on pulling the time behind one. A quarter past two will pass for half past, will even pass for three, on the theory that it is already well on the way toward it. The thirty minutes are taken as a sort of onset to the full hour from three to four, and inwardly discounted. In this wise the duration of the main rest period was finally reduced to no more than an hour; and even this hour was lopped off at its latter end, elided, as it were.'

32. Nietzsche, *The Joyous Science*, 35.

33. Rovelli, *The Order of Time*, 165.

34. Steiner, 145.

35. Steiner, 138.

36. *Perficio* in Latin means 'done completely'.
37. According to Everett, the Piraha lack notions of history (distant past) and an eternal God (distant future) because these concepts don't align with their focus on the immediate present. Everett states that the absence of history, creation, and folklore in the Piraha culture is connected to their unique linguistic perspective. Despite his efforts, he was unable to find any creation myths or stories about the origins of the world among the Pirahas.
38. Foucault, *The Order of Things*, 92. 'Rhetoric defines the spatiality of representation as it comes into being with language; grammar defines in the case of each individual language the order that distributes that spatiality in time.'
39. Augustine, *The Confessions*, Book IV (15).
40. Heraclitus, *Fragments*.
41. Bachelard, *Intuition of the Instant*, 6.
42. Kierkegaard, *Either/Or*, 43.
43. Plato, *Republic*, 173.
44. Encyclopaedia Iranica, 'Ahura Mazda'.
45. Rooted in the Greek verb *apollymi*, which means 'to destroy': Apollo is the sun-god who 'destroys' (separates) nothingness and chaos with his creative light of being and order.
46. Mithraists celebrated the sun's birth on December 25. See Harold Innis, *The Bias of Communication*, 70.
47. This is even more obvious in Russian, where *voskresenye* (Sunday) literally means 'resurrection'.
48. Moro, *A Brief History of the Verb To Be*.
49. Shakespeare, *Troilus and Cressida*.
50. The French word for 'now' is *maintenant*, which stems from *maintenir*, meaning 'to maintain'. It evokes the desire to hold onto time, grasping it firmly and never letting go. Similarly, the German word *Stunde* (hour) shares roots with the verb *stehen* (to stand).

51. In Latin, the prefix (in) is often used for negation (such as in-secure, in-satiable, or in-opportune). Thus, the *in-stare* here says that every instant of time 'stands by disappearing'.

52. Heidegger, *What Is Called Thinking?*

53. Rovelli writes: 'The good Lord has not drawn the world with continuous lines: with a light hand, he has sketched it in dots, like Seurat.' p. 75.

54. 'Seurat, just like Cezanne or Rouault', wrote McLuhan, 'are indispensable for understanding TV.' (*Understanding Media*)

55. Millions of tiny light bulbs behind our screens flash continuously, creating static images in every instant. These frame rates, measured in frames-per-second (FPS) or hertz, exemplify how moving time transforms into static images. We can also take the example of how movies work. A movie (what is moving) is originally called a 'motion picture' because its functionality is based on very fast-moving pictures — that is motion based on static images. The first movies were literally collages of many pictures stitched together in a sequential movement and lit up from the background.

56. Etymologically, the word 'world' is a combination of Old English words *weor* (meaning man) and *eald* (meaning old or aged). The 'world' is the 'age of man' — his time.

57. Bachelard, *The Poetics of Space*, 30

58. Cioran, *Anathemas and Admirations*.

59. Bachelard, 228.

60. Mann, *The Magic Mountain*.

61. Rovelli, *The Order of Time*, 39.

62. Lakoff and Johnson, *Metaphors We Live By*, 154.

63. Buonomano, *Your Brain Is a Time Machine*, 7.

64. Augustine, *The Confessions*, Book. XIV.

65. Augustine writes: 'There are three times, past, present, and future. This customary way of speaking is incorrect, but it

is common usage. Let us accept the usage. I do not object and offer no opposition or criticism, as long as what is said is being understood, namely that neither the future nor the past is now present.'

66. Heraclitus, *Fragments*.
67. As well as Spanish *dia*, German *Tag* or the Russian *den*.
68. In Greek, *horizon kyklos* means 'separating circle', where *horizo* is 'to divide', 'to separate' — another reference to the sun's diving, and defining power.
69. In virtually all European languages, this negation in the word 'night' originates from the Greek *nux*, which means 'the time when work ceases' or even 'the time of death'.
70. The West, or 'the Occident', is where the sun sets (*occidere* in Latin means 'go down'). 'North' stems from the Proto-Indo-European word *-ner*, meaning 'left' — that is on the left side when facing the sun in the Orient. 'South' derives from the Proto-Germanic *sunthaz*, meaning 'sun-side', where the sun's warmth is most potent.
71. Gaby, *The Thaayorre Think of Time Like They Talk of Space*.
72. Bachelard, *The Poetics of Space*.
73. Lakoff, *Methaphors We Live By*.
74. Nietzsche, 15.
75. Nietzsche, *Beyond Good and Evil*, 1. 150.
76. The noon, derived from the Greek word *'nun'*, means 'now'; it symbolizes the present moment that cycles in eternity.
77. Augustine, *The Confessions*, Book XIII.
78. Cioran, *Anathemas and Admirations*. 5
79. Heidegger's own term for 'clearing' in German is *Lichtung*.
80. Foucault, *The Order of Things*, 361.
81. Rovelli, *The Order of Time*, 175.
82. Cioran, *Anathemas and Admirations*. 21
83. Bachelard, *The Poetics of Space*.
84. Zweig, *Dostoevsky by Zweig*.

85. Heidegger's concept of *Da-sein* (literally 'there-being') is a quintessentially existential word, as it posits that being can only be there where the human being is.

86. It is highly likely Dostoevsky's own experience before his mock execution in his rebellious youth, right before the Czar pardoned him and let him live at the very last minute.

87. Plato, *Republic*, 173.

88. Kierkegaard, *Either/Or*.

Part III Forms of Informing

1. Nietzsche, *Beyond Good and Evil*.

2. In their tome *What Is Philosophy?*, Gilles Deleuze and Felix Guattari praise the idiot as the foremost thinker: 'The idiot is the private thinker, in contrast to the public teacher (the schoolman): the teacher refers constantly to taught concepts (man—rational animal), whereas the private thinker forms a concept with innate forces that everyone possesses on their own account by right ('I think'). Here is a very strange type of persona who wants to think, and who thinks for himself, by the "natural light". The idiot is a conceptual persona.'

3. 'When I mention a table', says Kahneman, 'without specifying further, you understand that I mean a normal table. You know with certainty that its surface is approximately level and that it has far fewer than 25 legs.'

4. Nietzsche, *Beyond Good and Evil*

5. Havelock, *Preface to Plato*.

6. Chekhov, *Ward Number Six and Other Stories*. 'We have books, it is true, but that is not at all the same as living talk and converse. If you will allow me to make a not quite apt comparison: books are the printed score, while talk is the singing.'

7. St. Augustine, *Confessions*, Book VI

8. Neil Postman, *Amusing Ourselves to Death*.
9. Etymologically, 'document' comes from the Latin word *documentum*, which signifies 'lesson' or 'proof', and it is derived from *docere*, a verb that means 'to teach' or 'to show'. So, the original sense of 'document' was something that instructs or provides evidence.
10. Mumford, *A City in History*.
11. Innis, *The Bias of Communication*.
12. Humboldt, *Linguistic Variability*. 13
13. McLuhan, *The Gutenberg Galaxy*, 138.
14. Ong, *Orality and Literacy*.
15. Nietzsche, *The Joyous Science*, 123.
16. Humboldt, *Linguistic Variability*, 144.
17. Derrida, *Of Grammatology*, 41.
18. Pye, *The Edge of the World*, 143.
19. *Legenda* means 'things to be read'.
20. Foucault, *The Order of Things*, 42.
21. McLuhan, *The Gutenberg Galaxy*, 166.
22. Foucault, *The Order of Things*.
23. Derrida, *Of Grammatology*, 302.
24. Innis, *The Bias of Communication*, 128.
25. Nietzsche, *Beyond Good and Evil*.
26. Ong, *Orality and Literacy*.
27. Nietzsche, *The Joyous Science*, 260.
28. Rosa, *Social Acceleration*, 248.
29. *Modo* in Latin means 'just now'.
30. Luhmann, *Observations on Modernity*, 3.
31. Baudrillard, *Simulacra and Simulation*.
32. Nietzsche, *The Use and Abuse of History*, 18.
33. Innis, *The Bias of Communication*, 79.
34. Le Bon, *The Crowd*, 109.
35. Steiner, *Real Presences*, 26.
36. Klemperer, *The Language of the Third Reich*, 15.

37. Calvin University, *Goebbels on Radio* (1933).
38. Klemperer writes: 'The German language only has one adjective corresponding to *Rede* (speech) and *reden* (to speak) — *rednerisch* (rhetorical), an adjective which does not have a particularly good ring to it, a rhetorical achievement is always open to accusations of being merely hot air. One could almost speak here of a distrust of public speakers intrinsic to the German national character.'
39. Diener, *LQI: Notre Language Quotidienne Informatisée*.
40. See Lakoff and Nunez's *Where Mathematics Comes From*.

Bibliography

Aristotle. *Metaphysics*. LaVergne, TN: NuVision, 2009.

— — —. *On the Soul: And, On Memory and Recollection*. Translated by Joe Sachs. Rev. ed. Santa Fe, N.M: Green Lion Press, 2004.

— — —. *Poetics*. Dover Thrift Editions. Mineola, N.Y: Dover Publications, 1997.

Augustine of Hippo. *The Confessions*. 1st ed. Vintage Spiritual Classics. New York: Vintage Books, 1998.

Bachelard, Gaston. *Intuition of the Instant*. Translated by Eileen Rizo-Patron. Northwestern University Studies in Phenomenology and Existential Philosophy. Evanston, Ill: Northwestern University Press, 2013.

— — —. *The Poetics of Space*. Translated by M Jolas. Penguin Books, 2014.

Baudrillard, Jean. *Simulacra and Simulation*. The Body, in Theory. Ann Arbor: University of Michigan Press, 1994.

Berlin, Isaiah. *The Hedgehog and the Fox: An Essay on Tolstoy's View of History*. Second Edition. Princeton, New Jersey: Princeton University Press, 2013.

Buonomano, Dean. *Your Brain Is a Time Machine: The Neuroscience and Physics of Time*. First edition. New York: W. W. Norton & Company, 2017.

Chekhov, Anton Pavlovich. *Ward Number Six and Other Stories*. Translated by Ronald Hingley. Oxford World's Classics. Oxford : New York: Oxford University Press, 2008.

Cioran, E. M. *Anathemas and Admirations*. Translated by Richard Howard. New York: Arcade Pub, 2012.

Dante Alighieri. *The Divine Comedy*. Translated by Henry Francis Cary, Claire E Honess, and Stefano Albertini. Ware (England): Wordsworth, 2009.

Derrida, Jacques. *Of Grammatology*. Corrected ed. Baltimore: Johns Hopkins University Press, 1998.

Diener, Yann. *LQI: Notre Langue Quotidienne Informatisée*. Paris: Les Belles Lettres, 2022.

Dostoevsky, Fyodor. *Crime and Punishment: A Novel in Six Parts with Epilogue*. 1st Vintage classics ed. Vintage Classics. New York: Vintage Books, 1993.

— — —. *The Brothers Karamazov*. Mineola, N.Y.: Dover Publications, 2015.

— — —. *The Gambler*. New York: Bantam Books, 1997.

— — —. *The Idiot*. Translated by Richard Pevear and Larissa Volokhonsky. New York: Vintage Books, 2003.

Ellul, Jacques. *La parole humiliée*. La petite vermillon 391. Paris: la Table ronde, 2014.

Encyclopaedia Iranica. 'Ahura Mazda'. Accessed 22 February 2022.

Everett, Daniel Leonard. *Don't Sleep, There Are Snakes: Life and Language in the Amazonian Jungle*. 1st ed. New York: Pantheon Books, 2008.

— — —. *How Language Began: The Story of Humanity's Greatest Invention*. First American edition 2017. New York: Liveright Publishing Corporation, a division of W. W. Norton & Company, 2017.

Foucault, Michel. *The Order of Things: An Archaeology of the Human Sciences*. 1st American ed. World of Man. New York: Pantheon Books, 1971.

Gaby, Alice. 'The Thaayorre Think of Time Like They Talk of Space'. *Frontiers in Psychology* 3 (28 August 2012): 300.

Gadamer, Hans-Georg. *Philosophical Hermeneutics*. Translated by David Edward Linge. Berkeley (Calif.): University of California press, 2008.

Hadot, Pierre. *The Veil of Isis: An Essay on the History of the Idea of Nature*. Translated by Michael Chase. 1. Harvard Univ.

Press paperback ed. Cambridge, MA: Belknap Press of Harvard Univ. Press, 2008.

Harari, Yuval N. *Sapiens: A Brief History of Humankind*. First U.S. edition. New York: Harper, 2015.

Havelock, Eric A. *Preface to Plato*. Digit. Repr. Cambridge, Mass.: Belknap Press of Harvard Univ. Press, 2004.

Heidegger, Martin. *Being and Time: A Translation of Sein Und Zeit*. SUNY Series in Contemporary Continental Philosophy. Albany, NY: State University of New York Press, 1996.

— — —. *Heraclitus: The Inception of Occidental Thinking Logic — Heraclitus's Doctrine of the Logos*. London: Bloomsbury academic, 2018.

— — —. *History of the Concept of Time: Prolegomena*. Translated by Theodore J. Kisiel. First paperback edition, (First Midland Book edition). A Midland Book 717. Bloomington and Indianapolis: Indiana University Press, 1992.

— — —. *On the Way to Language*. 1st Harper & Row pbk. ed. San Francisco: Harper & Row, 1982.

— — —. *Poetry, Language, Thought*. 20. print. New York: Perennical Classics, 2009.

— — —. *The Beginning of Western Philosophy: Interpretation of Anaximander and Parmenides*. Studies in Continental Thought. Bloomington: Indiana University Press, 2015.

— — —. *The Question Concerning Technology and Other Essays*. Translated by William Lovitt. Harper Perennial Modern Thought. New York; London Toronto: HarperCollins Publishers, 2013.

— — —. *What Is Called Thinking?* Reprinted. New York: Perennial, 2004.

— — —. *What Is Metaphysics?* Vachendorf: Jovian Press, 2018.

Heraclitus. *Fragments: The Collected Wisdom of Heraclitus*. New York: Penguin Books, 2003.

Homer. *The Odyssey*. Translated by E. V. Rieu and D. C. H. Rieu. Penguin Classics. London ; New York: Penguin Books, 2003.

Humboldt, Wilhelm von. *Linguistic Variability and Intellectual Development*. Philadelphia: University of Pennsylavania Press, 1972.

Innis, Harold A. *The Bias of Communication*. 2nd ed. Toronto ; Buffalo, NY: University of Toronto Press, 2008.

Kahneman, Daniel. *Thinking, Fast and Slow*. 1st ed. New York: Farrar, Straus and Giroux, 2011.

Kierkegaard, Søren. *Either/Or: Volume I*. Princeton, New Jersey: Princeton University Press, 1971.

Klemperer, Victor. *The Language of the Third Reich: LTI Lingua Tertii Imperii: A Philologist's Notebook*. Translated by Martin Brady. Bloomsbury Revelations edition. London ; New York: Bloomsbury Academic, 2013.

Kolakowski, Leszek. *Is God Happy? Selected Essays*. New York: Basic Books, 2013.

Lakoff, George, and Mark Johnson. *Metaphors We Live By*. Chicago: University of Chicago Press, 2003.

Lakoff, George, and Rafael E. Nuñez. *Where Mathematics Comes From: How the Embodied Mind Brings Mathematics into Being*. Nachdr. New York, NY: Basic Books, 20.

Latour, Bruno. *We Have Never Been Modern*. Cambridge, Mass: Harvard University Press, 1993.

Le Bon, Gustave. *The Crowd: A Study of the Popular Mind*. Radford, VA: Wilder Publications, 2008.

Levi-Strauss, Claude. *Wild Thought: A New Translation of La Pensée Sauvage*. Translated by Jeffrey Mehlman and John Harold Leavitt. Chicago ; London: The University of Chicago Press, 2021.

Luhmann, Niklas. *Love as passion: the codification of intimacy*. Translated by Jeremy Gaines and Doris L Jones, 2014.

— — —. *Observations on Modernity*. Writing Science. Stanford, CA: Stanford University Press, 1998.

Mann, Thomas. *The Magic Mountain*. Translated by John E. Woods. 1st Vintage International Edition. New York: Vintage International, 1996.

McLuhan, Marshall. *The Gutenberg Galaxy: The Making of Typographic Man*. 1st ed. Toronto ; Buffalo: University of Toronto Press, 2011.

— — —. *The Medium and the Light: Reflections on Religion*. Edited by Eric McLuhan. Eugene, Or: Wipf & Stock, 2010.

— — —. *Understanding Media: The Extensions of Man*. Critical ed. Corte Madera, CA: Gingko Press, 2003.

McLuhan, Marshall, and Eric McLuhan. *Laws of Media: The New Science*. Repr. Toronto: Univ. of Toronto Press, 1999.

Merleau-Ponty, Maurice. *Consciousness and the Acquisition of Language (Studies in Phenomenology and Existential Philosophy)*. Evanston: Northwestern Univ. Press, 1979.

Moro, Andrea. *A Brief History of the Verb To Be*. Translated by Bonnie McClellan-Broussard. Cambridge, Massachusetts: The MIT Press, 2017.

Mumford, Lewis. *The City in History: Its Origins, Its Transformations, and Its Prospects*. A Harvest Book. San Diego New York London: Harcourt, Inc, 1989.

Nietzsche, Friedrich Wilhelm. *Beyond Good and Evil*, 2014.

— — —. *Human, All-Too-Human: Parts One and Two*. Translated by Helen Zimmern and Paul V. Cohn. Prometheus's Great Books in Philosophy Series. Amherst, N.Y: Prometheus Books, 2009.

— — —. *The Birth of Tragedy: Out of the Spirit of Music*. Translated by Michael Tanner. London ; New York: Penguin, 1993.

— — —. *The Joyous Science: 'La Gaya Scienza'*. Translated by R. Kevin Hill. Penguin Classics. (London) UK: Penguin Books, 2018.

— — —. *The Use and Abuse of History*. Mineola, New York: Dover Publications, Inc, 2019.

— — —. *Thus Spoke Zarathustra: A Book for All and None*. Translated by Adrian Del Caro and Robert B. Pippin. Cambridge Texts in the History of Philosophy. Cambridge ; New York: Cambrige University Press, 2006.

— — —. *We Philologists: Complete Works of Friedrich Nietzsche Volume 8*, 2011.

Ong, Walter J. *Orality and Literacy: The Technologizing of the Word*. 30th anniversary ed.; 3rd ed. Orality and Literary. London ; New York: Routledge, 2012.

Ovid. *Metamorphoses: A New Verse Translation*. Translated by D. A. Raeburn. London: Penguin, 2004.

Pascal, Blaise. *Pensées*. Translated by W. F. Trotter. Oxford (England): Benediction Classics, 2011.

Plato. *Republic*. Edited by G. M. A. Grube and C. D. C. Reeve. Indianapolis: Hackett Pub. Co, 1992.

Postman, Neil. *Amusing Ourselves to Death: Public Discourse in the Age of Show Business*. 20th anniversary ed. New York, N.Y., U.S.A: Penguin Books, 2006.

Pye, Michael. *The Edge of the World: A Cultural History of the North Sea and the Transformation of Europe*. First Pegasus Books trade paperback edition. New York London: Pegasus Books, 2016.

Rilke, Rainer Maria. *Letters to a Young Poet*. Revised ed. New York: W. W. Norton & Comp, 1993.

— — —. *The Selected Poetry of Rainer Maria Rilke*. Translated by Stephen Mitchell. New York: Vintage International, 1998.

Rosa, Hartmut. *Social Acceleration: A New Theory of Modernity*. Translated by Jonathan Trejo-Mathys. New Directions for Critical Theory. New York: Columbia University Press, 2013.

Rovelli, Carlo. *The Order of Time*. London: Allen Lane, an imprint of Penguin Books, 2018.

Russell, Bertrand. *History of Western Philosophy*. (New ed.), Repr. London: Routledge, 2010.

Sartre, Jean-Paul. *Nausea*. Madrid: Alianza, 1994.

Shakespeare, William. *Macbeth*. New York: Simon & Schuster Audio, 2014.

———. *The Merchant of Venice*. New York: Simon & Schuster Audio, 2014.

———. *The Tragedy of Hamlet, Prince of Denmark*. New York: Washington Square Press, 1992.

———. *Troilus and Cressida*. Washington Square Press New Folger ed. Folger Shakespeare Library. New York: Washington Square Press, 2007.

Sophocles. *Oedipus at Colonus*. Translated by George Young. Dover Thrift Editions. Mineola, N.Y: Dover Publications, 1999.

Stanford University. 'Text of Steve Jobs' Commencement Address (2005)'. *Stanford News* (blog), 14 June 2005.

Steiner, George. *After Babel: Aspects of Language and Translation*. 3. ed. Oxford: Oxford University Press, 1998.

———. *Martin Heidegger*. Champs 174. Paris: Flammarion, 1987.

———. *Real Presences*. Paperback edition. Chicago, Ill: Univ. of Chicago Press, 1991.

The Economist. 'The World's Most Valuable Resource Is No Longer Oil, but Data'. 6 May 2017.

Tolstoy, Leo. *War and Peace*. 2nd ed. Norton Critical Edition. New York: Norton, 1996.

Wittgenstein, Ludwig. *Philosophical Investigations*. Translated by Joachim Schulte. Rev. 4th ed. Chichester, West Sussex, U.K. ; Malden, MA: Wiley-Blackwell, 2009.

Zweig, Stefan. *Dostoevsky by Zweig (Kindle Edition)*. Translated by Eden Paul and Cedar Paul. Plunkett Lake Press, 2012.

———. *The World of Yesterday*. Translated by Anthea Bell. Lincoln: University of Nebraska Press, 2013.

ACADEMIC AND SPECIALIST

Iff Books publishes non-fiction. It aims to work with authors and titles
that augment our understanding of the human condition, society and
civilisation, and the world or universe in which we live.
If you have enjoyed this book, why not tell other readers by posting a
review on your preferred book site.
Recent bestsellers from Iff Books are:

Why Materialism Is Baloney
How true skeptics know there is no death and fathom answers
to life, the universe, and everything
Bernardo Kastrup
A hard-nosed, logical, and skeptic non-materialist metaphysics,
according to which the body is in mind, not mind in the body.
Paperback: 978-1-78279-362-5 ebook: 978-1-78279-361-8

The Fall
Steve Taylor
The Fall discusses human achievement versus the issues of war,
patriarchy and social inequality.
Paperback: 978-1-78535-804-3 ebook: 978-1-78535-805-0

Brief Peeks Beyond
Critical essays on metaphysics, neuroscience, free will,
skepticism and culture
Bernardo Kastrup
An incisive, original, compelling alternative to current mainstream
cultural views and assumptions.
Paperback: 978-1-78535-018-4 ebook: 978-1-78535-019-1

Framespotting
Changing how you look at things changes how
you see them
Laurence & Alison Matthews
A punchy, upbeat guide to framespotting. Spot deceptions and
hidden assumptions; swap growth for growing up. See and be free.
Paperback: 978-1-78279-689-3 ebook: 978-1-78279-822-4

Is There an Afterlife?
David Fontana
Is there an Afterlife? If so what is it like? How do Western ideas
of the afterlife compare with Eastern? David Fontana presents the
historical and contemporary evidence for survival of
physical death.
Paperback: 978-1-90381-690-5

Nothing Matters
a book about nothing
Ronald Green
Thinking about Nothing opens the world to everything by
illuminating new angles to old problems and stimulating new
ways of thinking.
Paperback: 978-1-84694-707-0 ebook: 978-1-78099-016-3

Panpsychism
The Philosophy of the Sensuous Cosmos
Peter Ells
Are free will and mind chimeras? This book, anti-materialistic but
respecting science, answers: No! Mind is foundational
to all existence.
Paperback: 978-1-84694-505-2 ebook: 978-1-78099-018-7

Punk Science

Inside the Mind of God

Manjir Samanta-Laughton

Many have experienced unexplainable phenomena; God, psychic abilities, extraordinary healing and angelic encounters. Can cutting-edge science actually explain phenomena previously thought of as 'paranormal'?

Paperback: 978-1-90504-793-2

The Vagabond Spirit of Poetry

Edward Clarke

Spend time with the wisest poets of the modern age and of the past, and let Edward Clarke remind you of the importance of poetry in our industrialized world.

Paperback: 978-1-78279-370-0 ebook: 978-1-78279-369-4

Readers of ebooks can buy or view any of these bestsellers by clicking on the live link in the title. Most titles are published in paperback and as an ebook. Paperbacks are available in traditional bookshops. Both print and ebook formats are available online.

Find more titles and sign up to our readers' newsletter at
www.collectiveinkbooks.com/non-fiction
Follow us on Facebook at
www.facebook.com/CINonFiction